A STO[...]
THE FLIGH[...]

Fugitives!

Aubrey Flegg was born in Dublin and spent his early childhood on a farm in County Sligo. He began to write for children after a career as a geologist with the Geological Survey of Ireland. His first book, *Katie's War,* is about the Civil War period in Ireland. His second, *The Cinnamon Tree,* is about a young African girl who steps on a landmine. *Wings Over Delft* is the first book of THE LOUISE TRILOGY. It is set in seventeenth-century Holland and tells the story of a young Dutch girl's life and love while having her portrait painted (*Wings Over Delft,* was Bisto Book of the Year 2003/4, and winner of the Reading Association of Ireland award 2005). In *The Rainbow Bridge,* second in the trilogy, the picture falls into the hands of a young French hussar at the time of the French Revolution and tells how the girl in the picture influences his life. The third book of the trilogy, *In the Claws of the Eagle,* is the story of a violin prodigy, Izaac Abrahams, growing up in Austria with the picture (and with Louise) in the years leading up to and into the Second World War, to the period of the holocaust.

Fugitives!

Aubrey Flegg

THE O'BRIEN PRESS
DUBLIN

First published 2010 by The O'Brien Press Ltd,
12 Terenure Road East, Rathgar, Dublin 6, Ireland.
Tel: +353 1 4923333; Fax: +353 1 4922777
E-mail: books@obrien.ie
Website: www.obrien.ie

ISBN:978-1-84717-202-0

British Library Cataloguing-in-Publication Data
A catalogue record for this title is available from the British Library

1 2 3 4 5 6 7 8 9 10
10 11 12 13 14 15

The O'Brien Press receives
assistance from

Editing, typesetting, layout and design: The O'Brien Press Ltd.
Printed by CPI Cox and Wyman Ltd.
The paper used in this book is produced using pulp from managed forests.

I am the wind which breathes upon the sea,
I am the wave of the ocean,
I am the murmur of the billows,
I am the ox of the seven combats,
I am the vulture upon the rocks,
I am the beam of the sun,
I am the fairest of plants,
I am the wild boar in valour,
I am a salmon in the water,
I am a lake in the plain,
I am a word of science,
I am the point of the lance of battle,
I am the God who created in the head the fire.
Who is it who throws light into the meeting on the mountain?
Who announces the ages of the moon?
Who teaches the place where couches the sun?
(If not I)

[From: *The Mystery*. Amergin was a Milesian prince
who settled in Ireland hundreds of years before Christ.
The poem, from *Leabhar Gabhála*, or Book of Invasions,
was here translated by Douglas Hyde.]

Acknowledgements

I am deeply indebted to my family and friends for their help and encouragement throughout the writing of this book. I am particularly grateful to my wife, Jennifer, for reading and commenting on my manuscript at numerous stages. My thanks to her also for her company on my research trips, and her eagle eye for finding places – such as the priory at Rathmullan – which feature in my story. I have special reason to thank my young reader, Stephanie Johnston, whose brilliant suggestions really brought my story to life.

To Denis Conway special thanks, firstly for his riveting portrayal of Hugh O'Neill in Brian Friel's play *Making History* and secondly for his recommendation that I read Sean O'Faolain's compelling history: *The Great O'Neill*. This book and John McCavitt's more recent history, *The Flight of the Earls*, have been my principal sources. Donal O'Kelly's one-man show, *Running Beast*, also added to my understanding of Hugh O'Neill.

My thanks to The Tyrone Guthrie Centre for two productive periods spent at Annaghmakerrig, and to all the staff who maintain this most perfect of creative environments. To Michael and Ivan O'Brien, and to all the staff at The O'Brien Press, my thanks for their unfailing encouragement, their patience, and skill. Thanks also to Emma Byrne for her imaginative design of the book, its cover and illustrations. Most especially, however, my thanks to Íde ní Laoghaire, my editor, whose contribution to the creative process goes far beyond her meticulous editing.

Contents

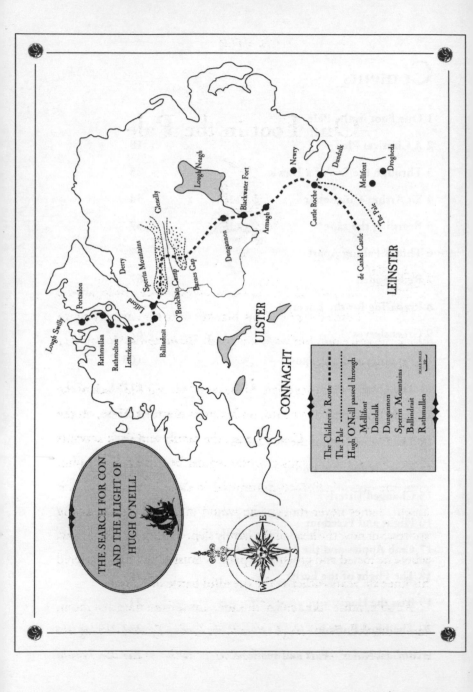

THE SEARCH FOR CON
AND THE FLIGHT OF
HUGH O'NEILL

Lough Neagh

Newry
Dundalk
Mellifont
Drogheda

Glenelly
Blackwater Fort
Castle Roche
The Pale

Sperrin Mountains
Dungannon
Armagh

Derry
Barnes Gap
O'Brolchán Camp
de Cashel Castle

Portsalon
Lifford
LEINSTER

Lough Swilly
Rathmullan
Rathmelton
Letterkenny
Ballindrait

ULSTER

CONNAGHT

The Children's Route
The Pale
Hugh O'Neill passed through
Mellifont
Dundalk
Dungannon
Sperrin Mountains
Ballindrait
Rathmullen

SCALE MILES

N
E
W
S

One Foot in the Pale

 ou could kill him, you know, said a voice inside James's head. He pulled his blanket over his ears, trying to block the voice out, but it was no good. *Slit his throat! It would be for king and country.*

James forced his eyes open. All he could see was the black of the night. He lay, stiff as a board, on his straw mattress. Here, on the upper story of the de Cashel castle, the family and their servants slept. He listened jealously to the regular breathing about him, even the occasional word murmured in sleep. Only Father was absent. James never thought he would miss his father's rasping snores, but now the head of the family slept in the great hall below, where he tossed and groaned in pain. A musket ball had shattered his knee six years earlier at the dreadful battle of Kinsale.

An alien snore, like a roll of thunder, came from the guest room. James bristled. *That's Hugh O'Neill, the Earl of Tyrone, sleeping like a lord. How dare he. It was he who dragged Father to Kinsale. I could kill him, easily. Take revenge.*

But James was too tired to kill anyone. At last he sank into exhausted sleep.

Con O'Neill, the Earl of Tyrone's seven-year-old son, was lying on his own mattress, scarcely a foot away from James, listening impatiently as the older boy tossed and murmured. Finally Con opened his eyes and looked at the boy. *Good,* he thought, *he's asleep; time for me to go.* A tiny square of pale starlight showed through the slit window in the castle wall. He must be careful. Too early and he might be challenged by the sentry, too late and he'd spend the day stuck in the castle being bored. He was used to sleeping in herdsmen's shelters, or even in the open under the stars. The night sky in the small window was calling to him like a song, but stronger still was the pull of his new pony.

Now! he decided. He got up with a deft wriggle, letting his blanket fall about his feet. He stood there, as he had slept, ready for the day, barefoot, in saffron-yellow shirt, dark jacket and breeches. All about him, lying on mattresses on the floor, were bodies wrapped in sleep, cocooned in light summer rugs. He stepped over the two boys, James and Fion; they belonged to the castle. He'd only met them the day before when he and his father, the great Hugh O'Neill, had arrived, unannounced as usual. Finally he stepped over the man-servant who slept across the door to prevent intruders. There was just enough space beyond the man for Con to open the door a crack; he slipped through this like a wisp of smoke, and was off, his bare feet making no more than a patter on the stone of the spiral staircase.

Ten minutes later Con was leading his pony from the stable. He had named him Macha, after Cuchulainn's favourite horse. He whispered today's plan into his ears. Never in his seven years had he come as far as this from his native Tyrone; it was a great adventure. But one adventure deserves another, and out there, less than a day's ride away was the Pale, the part of Ireland that the English ruled. He had heard so much about it. It drew him like a magnet, fascinating and terrifying, all in one. He just *had* to see it. But one thing was certain: it would be out of bounds to him, and he must be away before the grown-ups knew where he had gone.

As he rode from the gates he sat straight, aware of the eyes of the sentry on his back. His heart was fluttering like a sparrow in a cage. He longed to whack his bare heels into his pony's sides and gallop off, but he had told the sentry that Macha had a fever and needed to be walked in the morning cool, so he kept both himself and his pony well reined in. He could at least take deep breaths of the night air – free again after weeks of being good, and of attending to Father. A summer mist had settled over the meadow, and rose about him as he rode down into it. A warm milky scent and patches of deeper dark in the mist told him that he was riding through a herd of cattle that had settled on the road to enjoy the warmth stored there from yesterday's summer sun. He let the pony find his own way through the shadowy forms.

The road was rising now, lifting him out of the mist. He allowed his pony to trot, riding as he'd been taught, loosely and without stirrups, using his feet to urge, and to guide and to balance. At one point he spun Macha about and looked back. There was the castle, remote and secure. But he was free! With a whoop of joy he reared his pony into a half-turn, whacked him with his heels, and galloped off again on the road to the Pale, his pony a grey ghost beneath him in the dim light.

As he rode, he imagined the Pale as a high wall with battlements like a castle, lined with English knights in flashing armour, or perhaps peopled by blackened devils! Either way, he regretted that he hadn't brought a bow and arrows. His short little dagger with its jewelled hilt wouldn't impress anyone. He slowed to a trot, then a walk; it would be a long ride. He began to look about him.

Yesterday he had climbed to the uppermost turret of the castle and had quizzed the watchman as much as he'd dared about the Pale – how far it was, and how the land lay.

The watchman, glad to have someone to talk to, had pointed out the road to him. 'See how it takes a long loop to our left before it disappears into the trees?' Con nodded. 'It goes along that way for a couple of miles and then doubles back behind the hill that you see there in front of us.'

Con was surprised. *Why go all that way around?* Where he came from, people used pack-horses that could easily climb a small hill like that. All the time his father had been away fighting his wars, Con had been fostered to a family of herdsmen who followed their cattle and sheep from pasture to pasture. 'Why doesn't the road just go straight over?' he asked.

'It's carts we use here, son, and they need a wide, flat road. Then there's also getting through the forest.'

'Well, there's forest everywhere. That's easy.'

'Ah yes, but this is special – it's plashed. Thick as a thorn hedge it is.'

'Plashed?' asked Con, innocently.

'That's right,' the soldier chuckled. 'You ought to see those trees; we have them woven together like a basket. I tell you a sparrow couldn't get through that wood ... unless it knew the way,' he added with a wink. 'We wouldn't want Mr Chichester creeping up on us unannounced, would we?'

Con nodded wisely, but didn't ask any more questions in case he aroused suspicion. He ran his eye along the ridge. It was quite featureless except for a clump of Scots pines that stood tall and proud on a height opposite the castle.

Macha was a working pony and he soon settled into a pace halfway between a walk and a trot that he could keep up for hours at a time. Con looked about him, noting the way he was going, and imagining what he would do if he were suddenly attacked, and then imagining heroic deeds in which he always came out on top.

He whistled until his lips felt tired; then he tried a song or two. As the light increased, the grass began to show green instead of grey, and people appeared on the road heading towards him, bound for the castle – early risers carrying provisions and tithes, a pig perhaps, or some chickens hanging from a pole with their legs tied. This was a month of plenty when promises to the lord of the castle were kept and people paid their dues. Con made a cheerful sight in his bright saffron-yellow shirt. He had a greeting for all of them and they went on their way, smiling.

The sun was well up now, and he noticed that the people he was passing on the road were walking in the same direction as he. From the carefully packed baskets of eggs and the neatly tied bundles of vegetables, he guessed they were going to sell these at some market. There were a few carts and several pack-horses. Then, turning around a bend in the road, he saw a village ahead. It was the usual line of thatched cottages and a tower. Smoke was rising from breakfast fires. He looked left and right, wondering if this was the Pale, but there was nothing more than a ditch topped by a hedge, enough to keep out cattle raiders, no more. There was a town gate where a group of people had gathered while the gatekeepers questioned them and looked in their baskets before letting them through. As he watched, a couple of vagrants were turned away. Among them was a stooped man wearing quite the shaggiest mantle Con had ever seen. His hood was up, so that when he turned to glance over the crowd he looked exac... ing bear. The bear-man's head swung in Con's direc... though the face was shaded, Con felt eyes boring into h... immediate problem, however, was what to say to the guards i... asked him what business he had in the town. He was busy thinking up some colourful tale when a hand was suddenly placed on Macha's mane. There he was, the man in the cloak, looking up at Con, his eyes glinting darkly from his hood.

Con's hand flew to the little dagger that hung at his waist, but the man calmly put his hand on Con's and said in a low voice: 'Little lord, I'd hide your pretty dagger before it is taken from you.'

'Get away from me!' snapped Con, as he snatched his arm away, looking about for help. People were hurrying through the gate – in a minute he'd be left outside with the beggars and this strange creature.

Con slapped the bear-man's hand smartly with his reins and urged Macha forward to join the jostling crowd inside the gates.

———

'Make way for Milord Chichester,' came the shout. The crowd surged about Con, pressing back to make room on the road. The boy and his pony were pinned against the wall of a house. He could hear the beat of a drum and the tramp of marching feet. Then he saw, first a stickle of pikes swaying down the road ahead, then the pike men's shining helmets, and behind them a solid pha- lanx of musketeers, and the captain's match, a smouldering cord, looking from the butt of his musket ready to fire it or to light the matches of the other musketeers. Then came a dozen or so archers, their bows strung, quivers of arrows swaying on their backs. Finally, with a clatter of shoes on cobbles came ten or so cavalry officers, their plumed hats making a splash of colour. Con sat riveted, looking at them in amazement and delight. They were even better than he'd imagined. And suddenly, not five paces off, was Sir Arthur Chichester! This was the most powerful Englishman in Ireland. The man everyone feared. Only yesterday Father had told Con how that very man was trying to hound him from his own land, grabbing Irish land for English settlers, and forcing the native Irish to become Protestants. Indignation swelled up inside Con's small chest.

At that moment, as if the great man sensed Con's fury, he turned and looked directly at the boy; hard eyes flashed grim under his glinting helmet and his voice carried easily across the few yards to where Con sat. 'Where did that young dandelion blow in from?'

Why me? Con wondered. Then he knew; sitting on his pony in his bright saffron shirt, he stood out like a beacon above the sombre crowd about him.

A lieutenant riding a pace or two behind his captain looked across at Con. 'A pwetty girl by the look ... no ... no, it's a boy, that yellow thing's a shirt! The savage has dwessed up for you.' He sniggered. 'He looks harmless enough.'

But the general's face was cold. 'If you had fought these savages you wouldn't call them harmless!'

Undaunted, the lieutenant called out. 'Hey you, girlie, what are *you* doing on this side of the Pale?'

This side of the Pale! In a flash, Con realised what he had done. The Pale – he had crossed it! But where were the wall and the battlements, and the guards in shining armour? That glorified hedge he had seen on the way in, that must be the Pale. He had ridden all this way to see *that*! How could he have been such a fool? Of course, that was the reason for the gate and the guards. He sat there with his mouth open.

The lieutenant shrugged. 'It doesn't even speak English,' he said in disgust and rode on.

CHAPTER 2

A Classical Plot

 re ye going to lie there all day?' James opened his eyes, then hurriedly closed them again as a douse of cold water splashed across his face. Kathleen, Mother's maid, reached down and stripped the blanket off him. He grabbed at it, but it was gone. Then she stood over him, hands on hips, stirring him with her foot. 'Everyone's gone 'cept you, an' I've got the room to fix.'

James sat up, combing through his hair with his fingers. He looked over to the guest room and saw the open door. He nodded towards it. 'Where is he?'

Kathleen followed his look. 'Milord O'Neill's down with Sir Malachy.'

James remembered his night's torments. *I must stop thinking of him as 'Uncle Hugh', he told himself. He's Hugh O'Neill, the Earl of Tyrone, and no blood relation of mine! I am a de Cashel and we are Normans. We belong with the English. The sooner we break with O'Neill and the native Irish the better.*

He strode over to the water bucket and found it empty. 'Where's my water, Kathleen?' he demanded.

'I gave it to you a moment ago!' she sniggered.

James kicked angrily at the heavy wooden bucket, hurt his toe, and had to limp for the door. Kathleen's screech of laughter followed him down the stairs. *The cheek of her*, he thought, as he limped down. *Bloody Irish!*

Recently, James had been having secret talks with his tutor, Dr Henry Fenton. Dr Fenton had come to the castle a year ago to act as Father's secretary and as tutor to the castle's three children, then eleven-year-olds: James and his twin sister Sinéad, and Fion O'Neill, their foster brother. Every day they would have lessons in the great hall, where Father could hear them reciting their work. Mostly, however, Father would nod and doze, catching up on the sleep that his throbbing wound robbed him of at night.

Sinéad had taken an instant dislike to their new tutor and would re-enact the pompous little speech he had given them the day he arrived. 'My dear young nobles,' she would imitate, thrusting her hand into the front of an imaginary gown, 'like your Father, Sir Malachy,' here she would give an elaborate bow, 'I come from the oldest of Norman stock, and am a devout if humble Catholic.' She would copy her tutor's squirm, sending James and Fion into hoots of laughter. Then she would wag her finger. 'It's not me you must respect, but my gown, my degree in law', and she would stroke the fur of her imagined gown, explaining that it came from 'only the highest-born rabbit'.

In fact, Dr Fenton was a good teacher. At Father's insistence, he taught them through English, joking about 'knowing the language of the enemy'.

But two months ago, after a visit to Dublin, he had surprised them all by suggesting to Sir Malachy that James, 'as future head of the family', should come to his house for private lessons in Latin. Sinéad and Fion teased James over the 'head of the family' bit, but secretly wondered how James would manage. 'He can hardly remember the days of the week, let alone Latin!' scoffed Sinéad.

His first lessons had indeed been a misery. He could no more master Latin grammar than he could sew a fine seam. Sweat ran off him in rivers as he struggled with *mensa, mensa, mensam*. What did it all mean? *Why not just call it a table?* he groaned. Disgrace was looming – he'd be sent back to Father, a failure.

Then, quite suddenly, everything changed. Dr Fenton pushed his books to one side and said, 'I hear you are a fine swordsman, James?'

Bemused by the change of direction, James admitted that the Master at Arms had said he was quite good.

Dr Fenton beamed. 'Aha, I see the modesty of a knight in you!' James could only blush; he rather liked the reference to knighthood. Fenton went on: 'Let's forget the Latin, James. I just needed to know where your talents lie. I have a proposal for you. How would you like me to teach you about the great generals of Roman times: Caesar and Scipio – or Agricola, who brought the Legions to England, or Hannibal, who crossed the Alps with elephants? What d'you think, James?'

James's jaw had dropped. 'Oh how wonderful. But what about Father?'

'As we say in law, we must tell the truth, but we don't have to tell *all* the truth. This will be our little conspiracy, eh?'

Dr Fenton knew how to fuel James's imagination. In one lesson James would imagine himself in Roman armour leading his platoon through the sea-spray to conquer Britain, and in the next would be struggling with Hannibal in the alpine snows. On top of this was the added thrill of secrecy, not just from Father, but also from Fion and Sinéad.

About a month ago there had been a change. One day Dr Fenton moved his chair closer to James's and lowered his voice. 'Let's move on from the Romans, James, because, you see, we Normans are part of history too.' Over the next weeks his tutor gradually drew James into new and dangerous territory. 'It was we, James, who brought civilisation from France to England after the battle of Hastings in 1066. As a result, England is civilised now – but what about Ireland?' He fixed James with his slightly bulbous eyes. 'When the Leinster chieftain Dermot Mac Murrough invited us to come to his aid here, there were too few of us to civilise the whole of Ireland. We failed, and became more Irish than the Irish. So, you see, what the English are doing in Ireland now is really the work that we Normans left undone five hundred years ago!'

James was stunned. It was the complete opposite to what he had been taught. 'But – Father – Uncle Hugh – are they wrong to be fighting against England, then?'

'Yes, my boy. They belong to the old order, but *you* belong to the new. Think of the great generals I have been telling you about – they didn't become great by backing losers. You owe it to your father to think for yourself.' Again he dropped his voice. 'Do you want to end up like Hugh O'Neill, hunted from pillar to post like an old wolf? Do you want to blunt your sword cutting ferns for your bed? One day he'll be gone, and whose side will you be on then? With the squabbling Irish, whose only interest is to steal each other's cows? Or will you come out to support the English and King James, whose one wish is to bring peace and prosperity to Ireland? You won't be alone. While Sir Arthur Chichester leads the English side, you may trust him with you life.'

Just once the old rebel flared in James. 'I can't do this behind Father's back!'

But Dr Fenton had a reply ready. 'Of course, tell your father if you wish. You could always tell him in Latin.' James quickly forgot his scruples.

And now he had murder on his mind, at least when he was half-asleep! When should he confront Father and tell him O'Neill was no longer welcome? That the Earl of Tyrone was a loser? Fenton would know.

James set out for his tutor's house, weaving through the small town of thatched buildings that crowded about the castle tower. There were workshops – a forge, an armoury, a shoemaker – barns and stalls, not to mention the cottages and houses for castle staff and labourers on the farm. Closest to the keep were the kitchens, separate from the castle for fear of fire. Dr Fenton's house was just beyond the kitchens. 'Close to his dinner!' Sinéad had commented, eyeing their new tutor's bulging gown.

Dr Fenton always insisted that James come to his house only at lesson time, but James desperately needed his advice now. He knocked. No reply. Fenton wouldn't want him hovering outside, so he lifted the latch and stepped inside. The room was dark except for a widening wedge of light at the back. The tutor was opening the back door to someone else's knock. James could see him in silhouette, and beyond him a face James recognised: the pig-swill man. *What on earth could Fenton want with the pig-swill man?*

Now he heard the pig-man's voice. 'They're coming, Master!'

'Good!' Dr Fenton started to close the door.

'A shilling, your worship. You promised!'

A shilling! Is Fenton buying a whole herd of pigs? James wondered.

There was a brief argument, then the door closed and Dr Fenton turned into the room, smiling broadly and rubbing his hands. He saw James and started. 'Good heavens, James! Did you hear – no, it doesn't matter – you wouldn't understand. Why this sudden visit?'

'I've come to tell you, I'm going to tell Father that Uncle Hugh is no longer welcome here. It's time I stood up and–' He saw Fenton's face change from irritation to dismay, and stopped.

'James, dear boy, this is *not* the moment, truly it isn't. You see, I've just – you could ruin everything. Believe me, this is the very moment when we must make the Earl of Tyrone very welcome indeed. Great things are afoot.'

James, irritated, started to walk up and down. What was going on?

Dr Fenton seized him by the elbow. 'Calm yourself, James. You are like David looking for Goliath.' He had an idea. 'Why don't you practise on young Fion instead of the Earl? A little rough and tumble won't harm him. He is the Earl's nephew, after all. But you must go; I have business to attend to,' and he almost pushed James out the door.

Damn it, thought James angrily, *he's treating me like a child. But I'll have it out with Fion. He's had it coming to him.*

CHAPTER 3

Through the Eye of a Hawk

inéad had been looking forward to meeting Con, and was disappointed when she learned that he'd gone off without telling anyone. He had been asleep when she had gone up to bed and looked in on where the boys were sleeping. He was just a hump on the family-room floor, a flicker of red hair showing from the top of his blanket. Mother had been worried when he couldn't be found in the morning, and had made them search the castle for him, but when they told his father that they couldn't locate him, Uncle Hugh just said: 'Oh don't worry, he'll turn up! He has a new pony and I'll bet you anything it's gone too.' And sure enough, the pony was gone.

Con's father was 'Uncle Hugh' to the family, and a great favourite of Sinéad's. Usually when Uncle Hugh came, he would make time to chat to her and tell her of his latest adventures, but this morning to her annoyance, after talking to Father he'd locked himself away in the guest room saying he had to write a letter, and was not to be disturbed.

With her plans frustrated, she announced that she was off to the butts to fly her hawk and that the boys should come too as their birds needed a proper free flight. Flying the birds was an escape for her and a chance for her to imagine herself flying with them high above the castle. The boys joined her willingly enough. But when they got down to the butts and had put their birds on their perches, all James did was to needle Fion. Sinéad sighed.

She remembered the day when they were all just six, and Fion first appeared in their lives. Mother explained that the Earl of Tyrone had brought his nephew, Fion, to be a foster brother to James. It was quite a ceremony. The family gathered and the two boys were introduced. They walked around each other like terriers, with their hackles up, spoiling for a fight. Then, all at once, a strange man with flaming red hair and beard swooped on Sinéad, picked her up, and swung her on to his shoulder, saying in a loud voice: 'Hear ye – you boys – behold your sister, Sinéad of the Even Hand! Listen to her wise counsel or I'll come and beat the nonsense out of ye myself.' Everyone had laughed and the ice between the boys was broken.

That was the first time anyone had called her Sinéad, Irish for Jane, the name she had been christened; she thought it lovely, much nicer than Jane, so she kept it. That was how her friendship with Uncle Hugh began. Later, when Father came back from the battle at Kinsale with a wound that kept him on his couch for much of the time, Uncle Hugh was especially kind to her, telling her how valiant her father had been. He would come to the castle unannounced, night or day, and whether he stayed for an hour or a week, he never failed to ask for her.

'Where's my Sinéad?' he would roar. When she was younger he would take her on his knee, but he always talked to her as if she were grown up. He would tell her of the fine ladies he had met when he was in England, or of a wild-boar hunt on the shores of the lakes in Fermanagh, or of picnics and great feasts laid out on the ferns. She loved the rich Irish that he spoke, which had her dreaming of deep woodlands and wild mountains. He told her how her family, the de Cashels, were Normans who had come to Ireland as conquerors years ago, and how, in time, they had taken Irish princesses to be their wives, and so had learned the Irish language and Irish ways. In exchange, they had brought civilisation to wild men like him, which was the reason he had sent young Fion to live with them, so Fion could have manners put on him.

When Fion had first arrived, she and James had deeply resented the newcomer. The twins had got on fine together up till now and didn't want another of their own age in the castle. She and James did their best to make the poor boy's life a misery. But it didn't last long. In no time their old nurse was complaining that despite his devilment Fion could charm the birds out of the trees, and they were discovering that life in the castle was a lot more fun with Fion joining in. Fion was the one who had the wild ideas, while James was the one to carry them out. It was a good mix. Fion had the red hair and broad shoulders of his uncle; beside him James looked slight, dark, swarthy, and intense, a Norman to his fingertips. Sinéad had given up joining in their arguments, which were usually about boys' things anyway; she just patched things up afterwards.

***

Now she sighed. *Bother them! Wasting a good morning like this, arguing. Every day it's getting harder to get away from Mother and Kathleen, and those boys are just ruining it. I hate cooking, I hate sewing, and if Kathleen talks once more of a handsome husband I'll kill her. Come on, Saoirse, let's fly.*

For safety, the butts, where people came to practise archery, were outside the palisade that enclosed the castle and the castle village, so they made a perfect space for flying and training hawks. They were falcons really, valuable birds that had been trained to return to their owners and to swoop on their prey, sweeping down from on high to pounce on the lures the children threw for them. The birds knew the children's voices and would come on a call or whistle. Today, however, they were restless. They were disturbed by the boys' raised voices, and kept turning their hooded heads, as if longing to see what was going on.

Sinéad talked continuously to them, chirruping softly. Her bird, Saoirse, was a male peregrine, and therefore smaller and lighter on her wrist than the fierce females that the boys hunted with. The three birds stood proudly on their perches, their yellow claws digging into the wood. She talked to the females first; then she went over to Saoirse, and stroked his breast, watching the speckled brown and gold feathers spring up behind her finger. When her strokes had calmed him, she eased the soft leather hood from his head, and slipped her leather gauntlet onto her hand. He eyed her fiercely. Then, holding onto the light leather jesses that hung from his ankles, she encouraged him to hop onto her wrist. At last, with an encouraging whistle, she lifted him high, released his jesses, and tossed him into the air.

Up, up, up he went as she squinted into the sunlight, then up, up, up she went too, taking flight with him in her imagination. The voices of the boys faded. This was her escape from earthbound things. There was Saoirse soaring above her, waiting for her to catch up with him. Then, with a wild mew, he peeled off, circling the butts, and Sinéad could feel the draft of air that picked them both up as they soared away towards the castle. Nothing mattered to her now but the next stroke of his wings.

The grim walls of the castle – her home but also her prison – slipped away below her. A drift of smoke rose from the chimney above the battlements, where on its topmost tower fluttered the de Cashel flag, a single splash of colour. They soared higher and higher until the castle looked no more than a child's model below her. The polished armour of the watchman on the tower glinted bright. Beside him hung the Great Horn of the de Cashels – a bull's horn, too heavy to be carried at the belt, and as cracked as the sound it made. It had belonged to a Gaelic chieftain long before the Normans had set foot in Ireland, and had been taken by her father's ancestors as a spoil of war. Ever since the castle had been built, the horn had been housed in the tower, ready to be blown in times of emergency.

Sinéad imagined swooping down on the unsuspecting watchman and seeing him raising his cross-bow in alarm as she screeched past. *Oh no you don't!* She laughed as Saoirse swept out of range, but she knew he wouldn't shoot. Falcons were protected from the likes of him by both the English laws and the Irish Brehon laws. Falcons were a privilege of princes. In winter, when the wind hammered on the castle walls, or when Dr Fenton threatened to send them all to sleep, she would imagine herself flying, storm-tossed on some splendid journey, and she would be free!

From up here she could imagine the whole layout of the castle – the castle tower and the cluster of houses and buildings that made up the castle village. Around all was the palisade, a ditch topped with stakes hammered into the ground. This was their first defence against cattle raiders, but also in winter a protection against wolves that would happily run off with a lamb, or a chicken, or even a human baby. Outside the palisade was a circular mound ringed with hawthorn trees, where fairies danced on midsummer nights. Father told such scary stories about the fort that nobody – not even the boys – ever went near it.

Now for one last long sweep as far as the ridge with its clump of Scots pines.

The boys were still arguing below. Fion was at his wit's end. *What's the matter with James? He's been at me since we came to the butts, needling me, sneering at me. I'm fed up with him. I came down here to fly falcons, not to defend Uncle Hugh!* James wasn't usually a needler nor a jeerer, but he was being both just now. *One more jibe and I will flip,* and Fion could feel his anger rising, small tongues of flame seeking something to catch on to. *Where the hell's Sinéad?*

He called her name. No response. He turned, and there she was, standing at Saoirse's perch, head up, arms out, in a trance, a smile playing on her lips as she followed the sweeping curves of Saoirse's flight.

'Why don't you call her Jane? That's her proper name,' taunted James.

'Because Sinéad's the name she likes, that's why. I'd call you Séamus if you wanted – it's Irish for James.' It was just tit-for-tat, but it got to James, who was advancing on Fion, fists ready.

'Look, Fion O'Neill! I've had enough of your Irishness being forced down my throat. I'm James, James, James – and nothing else! I'm a Norman. Do you hear?' His nose was an inch from Fion's face. 'I'm finished with you, with your Uncle Hugh, and all your tribe. There's another way.'

Fion stepped back. 'All right, James,' he said, 'tell me. What's it this time? Who's the new Messiah?' It was a shot in the dark; James's new enthusiasms came weekly, but this was different. It was as if a portcullis had dropped between the two of them. A change was coming over James's face. His eyes lost their sparkle and became dark and steady, like water in a bog pool reflecting light but letting nothing in. Fion recognised that look: *So there really is something going on!* He was looking into the eyes of a fanatic. He shivered. When James spoke, he sounded like someone else.

'Us – us Normans,' he said, 'we're not Irish, you know, we never were. We came here from England, and that's where our allegiance must lie.'

Fion wasn't a proud O'Neill for nothing. Red anger obscured his sense and his vision. *Traitor!*

***

Sinéad was far away in her mind when the first fragments of the boys' furious exchanges began to get through to her. Then, to her horror, she heard the challenge: 'Choose your weapons!'

Duelling was taboo, to her an act of folly. She wrenched herself out of her reverie. Later she would think of her return as a giddying plunge from the sky, the wind tearing at her pinions; in fact, it took no longer than it took for her to whip about and face the boys. There they stood, white-faced and rigid, Fion pointing to the hawking gauntlet that he had just thrown down at James's feet.

'Pick it up, if you dare.'

Without taking his eyes off Fion's face, James bent and picked up the gauntlet.

'Your weapon?' demanded Fion.

'Swords, Mr O'Neill. Sharpened, naturally.'

'No!' she screamed. 'You can't, you won't ...' She rushed towards them, and then faltered as if she had hit a wall. For the first time ever, she felt truly frightened of them. 'Oh stop!' she cried, but she might as well have been shouting at the wind. The boys had moved into a world of their own. She watched them walk away. They were relaxed now, their differences apparently forgotten in the technicalities of a proper duel. This could not be real – but in her heart she knew it was. Neither of them would stop now, not unless *she* could find some way to stop them! Surely the armourer would never let them take out their real swords. But they were good talkers. They'd spin him some yarn. She shuddered: swords like razors! She must get help, but who could she turn to? Who would they listen to? Father? Yes, but he was too ill to stir from the castle. There was just one other possibility.

CHAPTER 4

Sir Arthur Chichester

s he looked at Sir Arthur Chichester, Con grew up. No longer was he just a young rascal riding out for an adventure; he was Con O'Neill, the son of the Earl of Tyrone. All summer Father had been talking about this man, Chichester, and how he had been hounded by him. Now, suddenly, here was the very man, riding out through the Pale with what seemed to Con to be a whole army. Where could he be going? Uncle de Cashel's castle? And if so, why? To Con it was quite obvious: *He's going there to catch Father!* His mind raced. *What can I do?* Here he was, jammed up against a wall. *I must warn Father – but how?*

He slid off his pony; he was far too obvious up there. *Dandelion indeed!* Head down, he led Macha towards the gate. The crowd had closed across the road with the passing of the horsemen, like water in the wake of a ship. People seemed much larger to him down at ground level. Con kept his head down and thrust into them. If they objected to being pushed aside by a small boy, they had to argue with the dogged pony that followed him faithfully, breathing down his neck. He could see the gates ahead; the last of the horsemen were just passing through. *Oh no!* The gates were closing, but Con wasn't the only one wanting to get out. There was a murmur among the crowd, early risers who had finished their business and wanted to get home.

'Stand back from the gates there,' shouted the guards, as they pushed the people back with the poles of their pikes.

'But we have to get out!'

'Nobody leaves here for one hour from now,' the guards shouted. Con, only feet away from the gate now, heard one of them explain to the other, 'He don't want nobody gettin' ahead and givin' de Cashel a warning.' The man dropped his voice. 'They've got O'Neill cornered at last.'

'Sir, sir,' Con called in English. He grabbed one of their pike poles and held on. 'I have to get out.'

'They all say that, son.'

'But ... but I have important information for Milord Chichester.'

'Le'go o' me pike, boy; he don't want to hear from the likes of you.'

'Lieutenant!' Con shouted through the narrowing gap between the gates. 'Let me come out. I have information for His Lordship!'

The lieutenant turned and saw him. 'Well, if it isn't Milord's dandelion. Suddenly found our tongue, have we? And speaking English of a sort too!' He wheeled his horse clumsily, dragging its head around as if it was cart-horse, and came back to the gate. 'Well, bwat, what have you to tell me?'

Con's mind was whirring. What information could he pretend to have? 'Sir, I have secret information for the general, sir.'

'Well, what is it?'

Con rolled his eyes towards the crowd behind him. 'I can't talk here, everyone will hear!' Indeed, he *was* afraid that some English patriot in the crowd would recognise him and put a knife in his back. Or an Irish one, if they heard what he had to say.

The lieutenant pouted. 'Tsch, I s'pose you're wight,' and then said to the gateman, 'Let him thwough. I'll see he doesn't escape.' The guards raised their pikes and Con and his pony were allowed through. 'Lead that cweature, boy, and come with me.'

Creature! Con was furious. *We'll show him, won't we, Macha!* For a wild moment he thought he'd make a break for it, but, truly, a pony is no match for a horse, and he would soon be ridden down. The soldiers were being formed into marching order under the watchful eye of the general while Con was being led forward. He'd have to say something now, but what? The general turned, caught sight of Con's yellow shirt, and a look of thunder crossed his face.

'Lieutenant Bonmann, what the devil are you doing with that boy?'

So that was the lieutenant's name; Con was sure he'd heard it somewhere before.

'He says he has important information for you, sir.'

The general growled. 'All right, bring him here, and if he's a nuisance, you can have the pleasure of shooting him, dandelion or no.' He glowered at Con. 'Come here, boy! Lieutenant, you can wait there.' Con walked forward, his knees feeling like jelly. 'D'you speak English?' the general demanded, leaning forward in his saddle.

'Yes, sir,'

'Well? What's your message?'

Con stood tongue-tied. Then, like a whisper, it came to him. 'Sir – Milord – I have secret information ...' He looked about him as if nervous that someone might hear, and dropped his voice. 'The Lord of Tyrone, sir, he's lodging at de Cashel's castle, sir!' *He knows it already, so it won't make any difference. He'll think I am on his side and let me go.* Con watched the man's expression. *Am I betraying my own father? Is this news to him?* There was surprise on the general's face, but it seemed mostly surprise that this new spy was a mere seven-year-old.

'Well, well, well. So how do you have this information, pray?'

'My sister works in the castle, sir,' improvised Con quickly.

'And does she speak English like you? That would be unusual for a serving girl.'

'She was in service in Dundalk, sir,' said Con, naming the only English-speaking town he knew. Still those cold eyes bored into him, but now there were sounds that the column was ready to move.

The general looked up. 'Bonmann!' he yelled. 'Take this lad. Let him ride, but hold his reins and guard him with your life. Put an archer on him. He may be telling the truth, or he may be use-able in some way or other.' He raised his arm, the drums began to beat and the column was on its way.

Con had no alternative but to hand his reins to the lieutenant, who took them as if they were twin snakes. He hooked them onto his saddle-horn.

'So, I'm stuck with you for the journey, then. What stowies did you tell his lordship?'

'I can't say, sir. It's a secret.'

'Oh, be like that!' Bonmann said petulantly. 'Archer!' he called. An archer stepped out from the ranks. 'One move from this bwat and you skewer him, all wight?'

The archer, who looked to have the brains of an ox, took an arrow from his quiver, notched it to his bow and fell in behind the two riders.

If only my English was better I might get some information from this Englishman, thought Con. He'd learned English from one of Mother's ladies-in-waiting, but this man had a funny way of speaking that made him feel uncertain. As they moved forward, Con measured the distance to the forest edge wondering if he would be able to make a run for it, but it was too far. He'd never make it to the forest before a horseman caught up with him, and then there was the archer; the thought of an arrow between his shoulder blades made him squirm. He turned in his saddle and tried the archer with a grin, but all he got was a threatening lift of the man's bow; no help there.

The drum-beat and the tramp of the men's feet on the road were like a slow pulse. As the miles passed, Con's chances of getting away, and ahead of the army to warn Father, were getting fewer and fewer. With every step, time was running out. He looked about him. He counted the men in the column and then looked at the pattern of their march. The general rode in front with two mounted lieutenants, and then came the pike-men, their pikes raised. Behind them followed the musketeers and then the archers. There were also a half-dozen cavalry, gentlemen all, who were probably supposed to march on the flanks of the column, but spent most of their time chatting and laughing to the rear. The only one who seemed in any way alert was General Chichester himself, who was constantly looking ahead and slowing the column as if he felt in danger of an ambush. Con imagined himself as the commander of an Irish force lying in wait for the column, and in no time he was chasing the whole English column into the sea.

He was suddenly brought back to reality. The column had stopped; but Con's reins were hooked over the lieutenant's saddle, so his pony was brought up with a painful jolt. In panic, Macha wheeled and backed away, pulling hard against his reins.

'Dwat!' shouted Lieutenant Bonmann, as his saddle, loose because he hadn't tightened the girth properly, slipped sideways on his horse's back.

But why had they stopped? As Con calmed his pony, he looked ahead. He could see a sharp bend in the road. Here, for the first time, the forest crowded close to the road. It was the perfect place for an ambush – but wasn't it also the perfect place for Con to escape? He could see Chichester at the corner, his hand still up to halt the column. He leaned forward. 'Come on, Macha, we'll go for it!' he whispered, and he grabbed his pony's reins from where they hung slack under his chin and heaved. Lieutenant Bonmann's saddle now tipped over, and he fell in a flounder of arms and legs. Con's reins slipped off the pommel of the saddle – and he was free. But the archer! Out of the corner of his eye, Con could see the man readying his bow.

'My Lord Chichester!' he shouted. 'Beware, there is an ambush!' His voice carried high and clear. The archer looked around as if for orders, but Lieutenant Bonmann was hopping around trying to get his foot out of his stirrup. There was only one safe direction for Con to go. *Ride for the general,* he thought, *the archer will never risk a shot in his direction.* Clapping his heels to his pony's sides, he rode straight towards Sir Chichester.

However, he had reckoned without Lieutenant Bonmann. 'Shoot him, you wetch!'

Con heard the command and flattened himself over the saddle as an accurately aimed arrow hissed above his back. He could see the arrow speed beyond him and for one heart-stopping moment he thought it would hit the general. Instead it fell short, causing the general's horse to rear on its hind legs.

'General!' shouted Con again. He didn't like the way Chichester was reaching for his sword. 'There is an ambush waiting!' He pointed at the corner. He saw a moment's puzzlement on the general's face. He was safe from the archer, who wouldn't risk two shots at the general, but Chichester had drawn his sword now. Confusion was Con's only weapon.

'Come on, lads,' he roared. 'It's Con! To the attack!' He changed direction and galloped for all he was worth towards the sheltering corner of the forest. Again he flattened himself along the pony's back.

Con galloped until he reckoned he was well beyond bow-shot and then turned. There was no sign of a chase. Not even Chichester peering around the corner. He gave a yip of triumph and waved his fist in the air. He patted Macha, whose sides were heaving from the gallop. The road was a temptation, but he knew only too well that he would be galloped down in minutes by the cavalry once they tumbled to it that his talk of an ambush was a hoax. He hadn't escaped from the army just to be run down by Bonmann wobbling on horseback. He must be careful. He must take to the forest now.

The trees on his left climbed to a long, low ridge. His eye ran along its spine. Trees, more trees, featureless trees – until there, rising above the leafy canopy, was a clump of Scots pines, straight, proud trees with bristle-brush tops. Were they familiar? They were! Con's heart gave a surge. *Of course! Those are the ones I saw from the de Cashel castle. Now I know where I am. The castle must be just over the ridge. Easy! I'll be over there and giving my warning in half an hour.* He turned and began to skirt the forest edge, looking for a path. There had to be one, it was such an obvious short-cut to the castle. He began to hum, making up a song about 'Bonmann the Bwave'.

He came on what he was looking for sooner than he expected. An old pack-horse road, if ever there was one. He turned into it, still humming, urging his pony forward. *Oh no!* There was a fallen tree across it. Perhaps the path had not been used for a while. He struck off into the trees to by-pass the fallen trunk, but immediately found his way blocked again. He'd never seen a forest like this. The young trees were bent over, twisted and plaited together like a basket. He dismounted and started pushing at the tangle, but this wasn't ordinary forest – it seemed to fight him, catching at his clothes. When he tried to back out, it seemed as if the branches had come alive, grabbing him at every twist and turn. *Oh, how can I get out?* His pony's anxious whicker showed him the way. Macha stood with his head on Con's shoulder and the boy stroked his pony for comfort. Then he remembered the watchman on the castle tower. 'The wood is plashed,' he had said, 'a sparrow couldn't fly through it!' Con could believe that now, but hadn't he added: 'not unless it knew the way'? *Oh yes!* Con thought, *but who's going to show me the way?* The only thing he could do was to retreat. When he emerged out of the forest he was dazzled by the sunlight – and the shouts from behind him told him that he had been seen. He shaded his eyes. The army had turned the corner – two horsemen were even now detaching themselves from the column and heading straight towards him.

For a moment he was tempted to give up. In another ten minutes they would have him, anyway, but then he remembered Father shouting, 'That man is hounding me!' and a flash of white-hot rage shot through him. He gathered his pony's trailing reins, scrambled into the saddle, and turned towards his pursuers with a yell of defiance: 'Come on, Sir Chichester, hound *me* instead!' Then he spun about and fled headlong along the forest edge.

He had no plan; he would never be able to find a path at this speed. He'd wait until they were close, then plunge into the forest, abandon Macha and perhaps wriggle through the plashing, though on foot he'd never get to the castle in time for Father to get away. He spotted an oddly shaped hump of hay ahead. *I'll ride that far,* he thought, *I'll make up my mind then.* And he rode like fury.

He was only yards from it when, without warning, the hump rose up out of the ground, and Con found himself holding onto his pony's neck as Macha reared in terror. A bear, was his first thought, escaped from some wandering performer, but no, it was the man in the shaggy cloak, the one who'd warned him about his dagger. Without any explanation, the man calmly reached out, took Macha's bridle before he could bolt, and led him and a very startled Con straight towards the forest edge. Con had his hand on his dagger, ready to slash and run if he needed to, but the clatter of hooves behind was getting louder. Every second counted now, and here he was, being led straight towards what looked to be an impenetrable hedge of hawthorn and bramble. Without hesitation, the lumbering figure – his guide or his captor? – parted a screen of elder that had sprung up in front of a fallen oak and led Con, still on his pony, into a green cavern behind the massive trunk. Con slid from the saddle. His new friend held a finger to his lips. The clatter of hooves on stone changed to the thud of hooves on grass as the horses behind turned in off the road. *Did they see us?* Con raised a questioning eyebrow. The man stepped forward and reached up to fondle Macha's ears. Hooves pounded on the soft turf just yards away.

A voice called out, 'I'm sure this is where he went.' Con started; they were so close. 'A sparrow wouldn't get through that bush, let alone a boy. You try the forest there.' Con looked anxiously at his silent companion as the nearby bushes began to shake. There was some lusty swearing. 'Here, Jake, come and look at this. Someone has twisted the branches together like a wattle wall.' There were more crashes. Then Jake's voice said: 'We'll never get through this. Let's listen; if he's anywhere around we'll hear him.'

Con had never heard silence like this before. He could hear his own breathing, his heart beating. His new companion seemed, miraculously, to have found some oats in his pocket and was feeding them to the pony. The crunch–crunch of chewing seemed loud enough to bring the whole of Chichester's army on them. Then one of the searcher's horses whinnied; Macha raised his head as if to answer, but in one deft movement the man enveloped it in his cloak. The pony didn't whinny, but he shifted his feet.

'Did you hear that?' But by now the tramp of marching feet, the clink of harness and clatter of hooves was loud enough to drown anything but an outright whinny.

'Let's forget it. The little blighter won't be able to get through here any more than we can. Anyway, he unseated Bonmann, and nearly got an arrow stuck in the general – I reckon we owe him one.'

The sound of their horses faded and Con and his new friend were left looking at each other.

'Thank you,' said Con. Then, in wonder: 'Who are you? I've been wondering ever since you warned me about my dagger. I'm sorry I was rude. Just now I thought you were a haystack!'

The man laughed. 'That'll do, I'm better without a name. A name can save a man and a name can hang a man. But here's a hint for you. I know you: Con, son of Hugh, son of Matthew, son of Con Bacach. I could go on … That's my trade. But I think you should be on your way.'

'And I thought you were a vagabond, but you are a poet!'

'The guard at the gate thought I was a vagabond too, and that's my disguise. But it worked out well because it meant I was outside the gate when Chichester came through.'

Con had seen poets before, but always as revered figures at feasts, telling tales of times past, playing their instruments, or singing songs. To be rescued by one was like Cuchulainn himself coming striding through the woods to his aid. The man, who had thrown off his cloak, was now standing straight, the stoop, apparently, part of his disguise. He was tall, dressed in simple clothes, but of the best cloth. His combed hair reached his shoulders. His trimmed beard jutted out to give his face a determined look. As he guided Macha through the plashing, he told Con which path to follow to get to the Scots pines, and, from there, the way to the castle. 'Are you listening, boy?' Con, who had been staring at his companion, nodded earnestly. 'Remember what I've told you, it's not as easy as it looks. If you don't get lost you will be there at least an hour before Chichester, but go carefully.'

'Thank you, thank you, sir. I could never have found my way through on my own.' A mischievous grin flicked across Con's face, 'Thank you, Mr Haystacks, sir!'

It wasn't long before he began to regret that he hadn't listened more carefully to the poet's instructions.

CHAPTER 5

Bearding the Lion

inéad had begun to run towards the castle when she
remembered Saoirse circling high in the sky. She put
two fingers in her mouth and emitted a whistle that caused the soldier on watch on the castle above to turn. To her pride and relief,
she watched Saoirse, a dot in the sky, turn and fall like an arrow in
a single swoop, to land a few feet from her. He stood there disdainfully, as if to say he had been coming anyway. She enticed him on
to her wrist, trying not to hurry him, and then from her wrist on to
his stand. Here she secured him with his jesses, stroking him and
praising him as she slipped on his hood. She hated to leave him
here, but she must hurry, and he'd have the boys' birds as company. At last, tucking up her skirts, she ran, taking shortcuts
through the huts and houses that clustered about the castle. A
chicken flew, squawking, from under her feet, and a woman threw
a pail of slops from the door of her house across her path. She
jumped over the stream of muck. 'Missed!' she shouted, and ran

on. When she arrived at the castle steps she paused to listen. She could hear the boys in the guard room arguing with the Master at Arms. '... but the fencing master said we could...' *Liars!* she snorted to herself.

She stepped into the great hall. The huge oak table, polished from the grease of a thousand dinners, gleamed in the pale light from the only big windows in all of the castle walls. The casements were thrown back to let in the air. A partition was drawn across the far end of the hall to form a temporary room where Father slept and held council with visitors and people from the estate. She listened; she heard a soft snore. No, she wouldn't disturb him. The only other person she could turn to now was Uncle Hugh, but did she dare? He was the one person, after Father, whom the boys would listen to. He'd been angry enough when he'd been disturbed over Con's disappearance that morning, and the servants were all in awe of him and his rages. But he'd always been nice to her, though that had always been when he'd been at leisure. She asked the guard if he had gone out, and was told no. She would have to be brave, so.

Gathering her skirts once again, she set off up into the gloom of the spiral stairs, moving in and out of the narrow shafts of light from the occasional slit windows.

She arrived at the fourth floor, panting, and pushed open the door to the family room. This was considered the safest part of the castle. There were three rooms up here, the largest being the family room, where most of the family slept and lived. Opening off this was the master bedroom, where Mother and Father used to sleep, but where Sinéad now kept her mother company, and then there was the guest room, now occupied by Uncle Hugh. Ominously, his door was closed.

Kathleen and Mairead, the two maids who were sweeping the wooden floor of the main room, were unusually silent. Kathleen, an incessant chatterer, put a finger to her lips and tipped her head towards the guest-room door. 'He's writing a letter!' she whispered, in awe.

They had been tidying up after the night, rolling up the bedding and putting it into the chests that, during the day, served as seats around the walls. Bright tapestries of hunting scenes covered the plastered walls. Even in summer a fire smouldered in the cavernous fireplace, useful for drying things, and for any small cooking jobs. Sinéad fixed her gaze on the guest-room door. *Courage! Now to beard the lion in its den!* She crossed to the door, trying to look braver than she felt.

Kathleen's eyes were popping. 'You can't go in there!' she mouthed. Sinéad made a face at her, raised the latch and pushed open the door.

There was a roar from inside. 'Can't you knock, wench!' She nearly fled. There was Uncle Hugh, bristling with rage, his beard and whiskers aflame in the light of the two candles framing him, one on each side of the table. In his hand was a ragged, well-sucked quill, its top bent over. In front of him was a sheet of paper, black with crossings-out. 'Oh, it's you, Sinéad,' he growled, jabbing the quill into his ink pot. 'Do you realise what you are doing?' He scowled dramatically. 'You are disturbing the Earl of Tyrone in a moment of history, writing to His Most Glorious Majesty King James of bloody England!' His voice was rising.

'I'm sorry, sir, it's the boys—' she began.

'Don't interrupt me, child,' he barked. 'I am writing to King James to tell him once and for all to get that dog Chichester OFF MY BACK!' And he hit the table such a thump that his quill went skittering off across his letter, leaving a comet-trail of ink-spots on the page. 'Now, look what you made me do!' He leaned back, fuming. Sinéad stood poised, ready for flight.

But suddenly he softened and turned his attention to Sinéad. 'Come, my dear, let me examine you,' which he did – critically – for a long moment, then he chuckled, and said in English, 'My not so plain Jane!' Then, back into Irish, 'But you have grown, my dear, you're quite a young lady! Come here, sit on the bench beside me. You're too old to sit on my knee now.' He sighed. 'Tell me about yourself.' The last thing Sinéad wanted at that moment was a cosy chat, but she knew her Uncle Hugh. She came around the table dutifully.

'So, how old are you now, Sinéad?'

'I'm twelve, sir. But it's about James and—'

He held up his hand. 'James is your twin, isn't he? *Ergo*, he's twelve too. He should be able to look after himself.'

'But not with *swords*, sir!' She bounced on the bench with impatience.

'Don't jig up and down, child. Just tell me, who is he squabbling with, and what they are squabbling about?'

'It's with Fion, of course.'

'Ah, so young James de Cashel, of ancient Norman descent, is having words with my nephew Fion O'Neill, who is ancient Irish – and, at a guess, the cause of the trouble.'

'Yes, I mean no, but Uncle ... please! It started when James said we should join the English!'

'Good lad!' Uncle Hugh stated. 'I've joined the English more times than I can remember. So?'

'He said that the English were honourable and would let us keep our lands and protect us from the "wild Irish" – and I think he means it.'

The Earl took a deep breath. 'I love the English, you know, Sinéad – their great houses and their fine manners. Didn't I spend my childhood fostered to an English family? And they loved me too, just as a shepherd loves the lamb he suckles with a bottle. But then – surprise, surprise – I found they wanted my fleece; they called me an Earl but took my lands, and now, damn it, it looks as if they want me as mutton chops as well.'

'Uncle Hugh, that's what the boys are doing now, making mutton chops of each other. They are taking sharpened swords from the armoury. Sharpened! You understand. *You* can stop them, I know you can!' She could feel tears brimming in her eyes as she turned to him.

'And I sit here doing nothing?' he said.

'YES!' she screamed, and launched herself at him, butting him and hammering at his shoulders as she had done when she was little.

All at once he stood up; the bench clattered back behind them and she found herself swept up and carried towards the door. 'Enough of your idle chatter, Sinéad! Damn King James and all his lackeys.' She held on tightly as he threw open the door. There was a startled squawk as Kathleen and Mairead, who had had their ears to the door, were scattered. Still holding Sinéad in his arms, he strode across to the top of the stairs. 'We're eloping,' he yelled at the open-mouthed girls as he set her down. Then, to Sinéad, 'Run ahead, my sweetheart, and clear the stairs for me.'

He unhooked his sword from the back of the door and followed her, bellowing, 'Clear the stairs for the Earl of Tyrone!'

<hr />

For a solid man, Hugh O'Neill could move surprisingly quickly.

'Well, where are they, girl?' he demanded as he emerged from the castle door. His change of mood was as sudden as their emergence from dark to light.

'In the exercise yard, sir,' she said. 'It's where they normally practise; no one will question them fencing there.'

'Well, lead on. Quick now!'

She darted off around the sheds and workshops that leaned

against the castle walls. The cobbler had left a bucket of water containing strips of shoe leather to soften outside his door. She sent it flying. He cursed her roundly – she shouted an apology, but ran on. The exercise yard was just beyond the forge. She heard clanging – *Dear God they've started!* she thought, but it was the armourer hammering out a new pike head. She flinched at the heat of his furnace as she ran past. When she came to the entrance to the exercise yard she slowed, frightened at what she might see. The yard was a rectangular space between the castle wall and the summer banqueting hall. It was reserved as a place for training the men in arms. She looked in. Thank God they were both still standing.

***

Against the towering wall of the castle, the boys, circling each other now, looked small and insignificant, nothing like warring warriors. They reminded her of the small fighting cocks that the men would set to fight each other while they laid bets on the winner.

Uncle Hugh was just behind her, watching the boys with interest.

'Uncle, the swords!'

'I see them,' he said in a low voice. 'Don't worry, they won't kill each other.'

'But they're sharp! Do something!' She grabbed his hand, prepared to bite him to get some action. He stooped as if to say something, but at that moment there was a clash of swords and he straightened and shouted out, 'Come on, James! Come on, Fion!

Close up, close up – get tore in there, lads.'

This time she did bite him. 'Stop them. Oh, stop them.'

He put an arm around her shoulders, but yet he seemed to be intent on the fight, like those horrid soldiers watching a cock fight. Without taking his eyes off the boys, he said to her, 'Watch the dust fly! It'll do them good.'

If the boys were surprised to hear his voice, they didn't show it. He, after all, was the very reason for their fight. With a zing of steel on steel, they closed. Sinéad watched a bright spark, struck from one of their blades, hang for a second above their heads as they reeled back from their clash. Then they went at each other like demons, cutting, thrusting and parrying. Now they were circling each other again, each looking for a way past the other's guard. No smiling, no courtly bows, just intense concentration. A strike above! A strike below! Both parried, then, with a grunt, they closed in, chest to chest, their swords crossed above their heads, the muscles on their necks standing out like cords. Sinéad could see Fion blinking as the salt sweat streamed into his eyes. She knew enough to know that the first to break would be wide open to a cut from the other. *Dear God,* she prayed, *please don't let either of them be hurt or killed.*

Uncle Hugh watched intently. 'Look,' he whispered, 'watch Fion's blade. James is trying to get it into the notch on his sword – if he does, he'll disarm him.' Sinéad felt as if her eyes were welded to those two crossed blades. Despite his efforts to hold it back, Fion's blade was being forced inexorably closer and closer to the hilt of James's sword. There – she heard it! A click! James gave a mighty wrench – and Fion's blade was flying through the air, broken off at the hilt. The boys reeled apart. Fion, smiling, looked ruefully at his broken hilt.

Sinéad let out a whoop of sheer relief. Now, surely, the quarrel was over. She looked up at Uncle Hugh and was taken aback to see a look of thunder on his face.

'Well, don't just stand there, James,' he roared. 'You have disarmed your man. This is not war – give him the victor's touch. Your quarrel is over, boys. We don't want bad blood remaining between you.' Sinéad remembered this ritual at games, how the winner would touch the shoulder of the loser with his sword, confirming that he had won, but also as a sign of honour and respect that told the world the quarrel was over. Sometimes they would even embrace.

Fion was waiting. James, however, was breathing heavily, as if struggling with indecision. Then, without acknowledging Fion in any way, he threw his sword into the dust of the exercise yard and shouted, 'That was no fight! Keep your toys!' – and he walked away.

Sinéad watched Fion's face drain of blood. She ran a few steps forward, trying to fill the gap between them, her arms out. But the damage was done. Fion also turned to leave, but in the opposite direction to James. Mystified by what James had said about toys, she walked over, carefully picked up his sword and felt its edge. It was as blunt as a piece of wood – it was only a practice sword. So the Master at Arms had refused them their sharpened blades. She turned to Uncle Hugh. 'You knew!' she accused.

'Yes,' he said, spreading his hands. 'I knew the moment we walked in. I let them at it because I thought it would be the end of their quarrel, but now I'm not so sure. There is more to this spat than meets the eye.' He frowned deeply. 'You told me about their quarrel, Sinéad. It seems to run very deep. Is it possible that there's a rotten apple here in the castle, someone who has been whispering in your brother's ear?' She shook her head, wrinkling her nose involuntarily. He laughed. 'Rotten apples don't always smell, you know.'

'I can't think of anyone, Uncle,' she said.

He nodded slowly and said, more to himself than to her, 'It could be a sign.'

'A sign?' she questioned.

Uncle Hugh looked at her and smiled, but it was a smile that had more sadness than gaiety in it. He touched her cheek, and said, 'A sign that your old Uncle Hugh should go somewhere and think.'

He turned and she watched him walk away, suddenly an old man carrying something heavy on his back.

CHAPTER 6

Things Falling Apart

inéad stood bewildered, alone and deserted in the exercise yard. She took a few steps after James but hesitated; then she turned to follow Fion, but faltered again. This was a boy's quarrel. *But why was Uncle Hugh so upset when they wouldn't make it up?* She made peace with the cobbler whose bucket she had knocked over, but being good didn't make her feel any better. There were chores to be done, but Uncle Hugh remained in her mind, his broken look, his hunched walk. Eventually she said to herself, *I'll find him, and I'll find out!*

Dodging places like the kitchen and laundry, where Mother might be directing affairs, she slipped into the castle and hurried up the spiral stairs. There was no one in the guest room. *Where's he hiding?* she wondered. *Try the battlements.* She went back to the stairs and followed the spiral up to the roof.

When she stepped out into the bright sunshine of the castle top she looked around. In front of her the slated roof stretched the width of the castle, like an up-turned boat. The slates sloped down on each side to a narrow walkway which ran right around inside the battlement, a low wall over which soldiers could shoot arrows or even fire muskets down on invaders below. Every few feet, the wall was built up high to make a shelter behind which the defenders could hide from the enemy. She was considering climbing to the turret where the watchman would be standing when she saw, half-concealed by a battlement, the familiar figure of Uncle Hugh leaning on his elbows staring out over the fields and forest below. She couldn't see his face for the gorse-bush fuzz of his beard and hair. At another time she would have tiptoed towards him and pounced on him, or pretended to push him over from behind, but now something held her back. The broad shoulders were shaking as if he was laughing; it was then that she heard a sound – a small, deep sound that made her want to back away: *Surely Uncle Hugh can't be crying?* She turned to go, but in doing so she clicked one of the slates on the roof, and heard his voice, as thick as leaves on a forest floor.

'Don't go, child, I know you're there.' He took out an enormous handkerchief, buried his face in it, and blew loudly. 'Come, there's room for you beside me.' And he moved over to make room for her between the battlements. She came and rested her elbows on the warm stone and looked down on the familiar scene below. This was where she had learned to imagine herself flying like Saoirse. She looked at Uncle Hugh and followed his gaze out to the place they called the 'gathering ground'. It had been one mass of men that dreadful day a few years ago when they had gathered to head for Kinsale where the Spanish had landed to help them fight the English. Black and gold, saffron cloaks and kilts swaying like daffodils in a merry dance. The de Cashel soldiers mixed in with the Gaelic tribes. Beside them the awesome Gallowglasses – warriors for hire – huge men with long hair and body-long battleaxes.

'They have all sworn to die rather than surrender,' Fion had said in awe.

Then came the cavalry, with mail coats and flashing breastplates of steel.

'Our cavalry are better than yours,' James had boasted to Fion. 'We have stirrups for our feet. Your lot just fall off in a charge.'

There'd been a brisk scuffle.

The bulk of the army was made up of kerns, foot soldiers with swords, and spears that they could throw to split a wand at twenty paces. But most exciting of all for the boys were the troops of musketeers. Sinéad remembered clasping her ears as they fired off a volley to clear their barrels.

Uncle Hugh turned to look at her now. 'Do you remember them, all those men – those brave men, Sinéad?' She nodded. 'Well, that winter I took them off to war. I walked them the length of Ireland like heroes, through rain and frost, all the way down to Kinsale. We had the English trapped, and if we'd had patience we could have starved them out in a few days – they had no food, you see. But Red Hugh said, "Attack them!"' He sighed. 'I loved young Red Hugh O'Donnell like a son, and I gave in to him. In two hours we had lost the battle and half the brave lads that you saw down there were dead. Isn't it right that I should weep for them?' Sinéad pressed close to him, and he put his arm around her shoulders. 'Now we're back to our bad old ways, fighting each other while the English stir the pot. Divide and rule. And we fall for it every time.' He sighed. 'Seeing the boys fighting just now brought it all back to me. I let them fight as a way to make up their quarrel, but it didn't work. Perhaps the old ways don't mean anything any more? Perhaps there is more to their quarrel than meets the eye?' He turned and looked into the distance. 'They're good lads, Sinéad, you must find out what's between them. Remember Sinéad of the Even Hand?' He chuckled. Then, clapping his hand to his forehead, he said, 'Damn me! I nearly forgot; I've left a small gift for you with your mother. I hope it fits.'

'Fits?' wondered Sinéad.

<hr/>

'Holy Mother of God! Sinéad! Where *have* you been? And *look* at the state of you, burned by the sun, your complexion ruined.' Her mother held out her hands in despair. 'And just when Uncle Hugh has brought you a present from Aunt Cathcrine.'

'Oh, what is it?' exclaimed Sinéad.

'It's a dress for a young lady, not that you'll ever be one at this rate!'

'Oh show, show me!'

'No indeed, not till you've washed. If your father was himself he'd beat your backside for looking as wild as you do.'

Sinéad skipped off. *A dress from Aunt Catherine!* she thought happily. When she came back, the dress had been laid out for her by the dressmaker. She stood dumfounded, her mouth open. Mother was right; no child's frock this, but a real dress for a lady!

'Mother, it's beeeauuutiful!' *What is that colour? The colour of heather in bloom,* she decided. 'And look – oh Mother, look! There are tiny flowers embroidered inside the pleats.' Tomboy that she was, Sinéad loved to dress up; people had even said she was pretty. Apart from her reflection in puddles, she'd only seen little bits of herself at a time reflected in her mother's tiny silver hand-mirror. In no time, she was standing on a stool while the dressmaker adjusted the length of the skirt. She gazed down, watching the colour on the silk change as the dressmaker tweaked and adjusted its folds. She ran her fingers between the pleats to feel the wonderful smoothness of the silk and slight roughness of the embroidery.

'This will last you well,' said Mother with satisfaction, as the dressmaker put a tuck into the bodice, which was close-fitting with long sleeves. At the shoulders were two little lace ruffs, with a larger ruff, like a small wheel, about her neck; it tickled her chin as she looked down. *It would be fun to look like a lady.* She chuckled as she remembered how Uncle Hugh had swept her up and carried her across the room. They all knew the story of how, years ago, he'd eloped with Mabel Bagenal; then poor, pretty Mabel had died – it seemed a shame. *Oh but it would be fun to elope …*

'Will you stand still, miss? How can I get your length if you twist about so?' grumbled the dressmaker.

When the dressmaker went off to sew the new hem, Sinéad, in clean day-clothes, made for the door. She had remembered that she'd abandoned Saoirse down at the butts, but her mother saw her heading off.

'Oh no you don't, young miss! I want rosemary and thyme from the garden, and you're the only one who knows thyme from a turnip around here.' Sinéad sighed, but it was a pleasant assignment.

When she'd picked her two bouquets of herbs she walked back through the orchard to see if the apples were ripening, but they were still green. She picked up a windfall; it looked perfect, apart from a tiny round hole. No rotten apple here, but it made her think of Uncle Hugh. *Surely there are no rotten apples in the castle?* She imagined a cloak-and-dagger figure. *Where would he hide, for a start? We know everyone here.* She dropped the apple into her apron pocket, delivered her bouquets of herbs without being caught again, and set off for the butts. *I bet the boys have forgotten the falcons; perhaps they've made up their quarrel.*

When Sinéad arrived at the butts, she had a moment of panic. Saoirse was missing! But then, so too was Fion's Granuaile. *I know ... Fion's come, rescued Granuaile, and out of kindness Saoirse, but he's left James's falcon for him to retrieve himself.* She sighed. *No sign of peace here.* Her gauntlet was lying on the ground, so she put it on and coaxed James's fierce female onto her wrist.

The falconry was a lean-to building against the castle wall. It was open to one side but had a loft above it, where the falconer kept all the gear he required for training and hunting the birds of prey. Under the loft, sheltered from rain and snow, stakes had been driven into the ground to make perches on which the birds were lightly chained. At night they would be carried back and put in the individual cages that hung on the wall. Dr Fenton had given the children a rhyme to learn in English:

> *An eagle for an emperor, a gyrfalcon for a king,*
>
> *a peregrine for a prince, a saker for a knight,*
>
> *a merlin for a lady, a goshawk for a yeoman,*
>
> *a sparrow hawk for a priest, and a kestrel for a knave.*

Sure enough, Saoirse and Granuaile were on their perches, but there was no sign of Fion. She was just easing James's bird onto its perch when she heard a low whistle, two notes on a descending scale. It was a secret call they used between each other, but where had it come from? She looked about her; there it was again! She looked up; it seemed to have come from above. Fine dust fell from one of the cracks in the ceiling. Whoever it was must be in the loft above.

'Fion? James?' she called.

'Shhh. Is James about?' That was Fion's whisper!

'No.'

'Come up here; use the ladder in the corner.' Sinéad had often wondered what lay above in the loft, but the falconer was as touchy as his birds, and she had never been invited up; now she climbed the ladder with interest. A hand reached out to help her over the lip into the loft. 'This is my hide-away,' Fion whispered.

'To hide from me?' she asked, a little miffed.

'Sometimes,' he chuckled. 'James – your father – everybody. Falconer is an old friend.' Sinéad knew this; Fion could make friends with anyone. She looked around at the lines of hooks hung with leashes and lures, bells and hoods. There were spare blocks and perches stacked against the wall and a wooden slab like a butcher's for cutting up meat and game for the birds. 'Come over and sit down,' Fion invited. He had made a nice space for himself. There was a seat made from an old board covered with sacks to make it comfortable. Light filtered between the uneven slates of the roof, but a rush-light also cast a homely circle of light on the floor.

'I'm going to leave the castle, Sinéad.'

'Oh no, Fion! Why? It's your home,' she said indignantly.

'It's like this,' he said. 'If James challenges me again, I will have to fight him. He doesn't want Uncle Hugh here, and that means me too.'

'Are you afraid of him?'

'I am afraid, but not *of* him; I'm afraid *for* him. You see ... I might win next time.'

'But then you could make it up, surely?'

'Not if I'd killed him.' A shudder went through Sinéad. 'If we fight again it will be one or the other of us. You saw, he had me fairly beaten and I was ready to forget the cruel things he'd been saying, but he wouldn't let me. He refused me the victor's touch. I must either take myself off or be prepared to fight again.' She thought of the triangle of friendship that had held them together for six whole years.

'Do you really hate him, Fion – hate us, hate *me*?' She put her hand in her pocket and took out the apple she had picked up in the orchard and began polishing it on her apron.

'Oh don't be silly! How *can* you say a thing like that? We three have grown up as one; we should be side by side, shoulder to shoulder, not enemies! I tell you though, something or somebody is getting at James.'

'Uncle Hugh said the same – that there might be a rotten apple in the castle. But surely we'd know? Rotten apples stink.'

Fion held out his hand. She gave him her apple; he turned it round and round, mulling things over. Then he asked, 'Mind if I cut this?'

'It'll be sour as hell.' She screwed up her mouth, but he went ahead, and cut the apple in two using his dagger. He gave a snort of satisfaction, and held out one half for Sinéad to see. There in the core, surrounded by brown dust, was a cavity, and in it was a small, white worm.

'Yuck!' she whispered. 'But who ...?'

'I think I know. Who does James visit almost daily on his own? Who would be fool enough to try to teach our James Latin? Or to imagine him as a lawyer, or a priest? No, Sinéad, he's not learning Latin, he's being groomed as an English puppet by our respected tutor, *Dr* Fenton! Fenton's our worm.'

Sinéad gazed at the apple. 'He looks comfortable in there, doesn't he?'

'So he should; your father clothes him, feeds him, pays him, all on top of what the English pay him as well. The only trouble is—'

'We don't have a morsel of proof. Do you think James knows?'

'That Fenton's a spy?'

'Yes.'

'Well, if he knows that Fenton's a spy, that makes him a spy himself – two worms in our apple. We must find him and confront him. But I can't because it would just end in a duel. Please, Sinéad, I don't want to believe this of James. But I'm afraid for him – and for you all.'

CHAPTER 7

Red-handed

eep in the forest, Con was lost. He couldn't believe it. He had been in and out of forests since he could walk; he *couldn't* be lost! But he was. And it had looked so simple from the road, just a short ride up to the Scots pines and down to the castle on the other side of the ridge. But which ridge? Which way to turn? Con's groan turned into something close to a whimper. Haystacks had said: 'Just keep to the track.' But then the silly old track had wandered off in a stupid direction, and the obvious route had been to strike up along this ridge. He had ridden confidently, expecting to see the pines ahead at any moment. After a while, though, the ridge had melted into the hillside, and small cliffs and dense patches of brush-wood forced him lower and lower down the slope. Then the trees had closed over him, blocking out the light. Great branches swept low across his path, turning him first left and then right, until he didn't know which way to turn. He couldn't go up, he couldn't go back. The only thing that had any meaning was the slope of the ground. He slipped from his saddle and walked, feeling the dip with his feet. He held his pony's head to his shoulder, telling Macha not to worry, that they would be safe if they stayed together. All he needed was to see the sun. From time to time he'd wipe his tears off on the pony's mane.

⟨━━━━━⟩

It wasn't the sun that finally gave Con his bearings in the forest, but a tangle of interwoven branches across his path. Plashing! He stared at the tangle ahead in disbelief, beyond it was – the road! By turning off the path too soon, he'd been forced all the way back down to the road again. He looked about him. It seemed clearer here and he soon saw the reason: in plashing the forest edge, a strip of woodland behind had been cleared of undergrowth. With a lithe movement he was in the saddle again, his shameful tears dried and forgotten. He trotted briskly along, parallel to the road, his eyes searching the ground. If there had been one path, surely there'd be another? But how much time had he lost? Was the army ahead or behind? Was Chichester even now approaching the castle?

There it was! A path, little used, but cut clear, running straight up to the ridge. He leaned forward, whispered magic words into Macha's ears, brought his hard little heels down on the pony's sides and they were off up the steep path.

Sinéad wasn't sure she really *wanted* to find James. It would be difficult to talk to him, especially if he was in one of his moods. There was only one place she knew of that he used as a hideaway, simply because it was difficult to get to. It was in the store-rooms in the undercroft of the castle, and getting in was an awkward climb over the door. She looked at her clean apron and sighed – more trouble for her if this one got dirty.

When she got to the castle, however, she saw to her relief that the doors were open to let in the first sacks of grain from the harvest. Men from the fields were tipping barley in golden streams into the huge wooden bins that lined the walls. There had to be enough food stored in the castle to keep not just the family, but the whole garrison, for a month or more if the castle was besieged. She followed the men in. Green-eyed cats on high alert for any disturbed mouse or rat ignored her as she passed, their tails twitching. These cats were wild as small tigers, definitely not for petting. She tried to look casual, poking among the barrels laid out ready to be filled with salted meat for the winter. Above in the arched stone roof were rows of hooks to take hams, smoked sides of bacon and even whole beef carcasses. She tapped on the barrels of Spanish wine to see if they were full. When she found a loose bung on a barrel she pulled it out and wrinkled her nose at the sharp smell: wine turned to vinegar, it would probably be used for pickling now. More rewarding was a tub of honey that was leaking a line of small golden droplets, so she ran her finger along the seam. Then, realising that the men had left, she climbed quickly up over sacks of dried peas and down into the corner where James had his retreat. She noticed fresh earth, which was strange, but no James. She was wondering where to look next when she noticed the light dimming; the doors were beginning to close. She leapt down over the sacks and threw herself through the closing crack, and emerged to shouts of laughter from the men outside.

'Watch out, lads, the ferret's after her!'

'Have you seen James?' she asked, airily.

'No, miss. Not since he was looking for the armourer earlier.'

There was nothing for it but to search the castle. This was the quiet part of the day when people took a rest. The soldier in the guard room had only just come on duty, but he hadn't seen James. The great hall was silent so she tiptoed across it and peered behind Father's screen. His desk was covered with papers, where a single candle burned. There was no sign of Father. She was just backing out when Dr Fenton's face lifted suddenly out of the blackness from beyond the candle. She stepped back in fright, then pulled herself together. *He has every right to be here. He is Father's secretary, after all.* She managed a smile. As she backed away, she could feel her heart pattering like a drum. *I mustn't get silly about this!* She worked her way up from floor to floor, avoiding only the soldiers' quarters, but they assured her that James was not there.

When she arrived at the family rooms at the top of the castle, she found them deserted. Mother's door was closed; she glanced in, but it was empty. Uncle Hugh's door was wide open; he must still be up on the battlements. That left just one place to be searched on this floor.

Holding her breath, she pushed aside the heavy curtain to the garderobe – the toilet – where the winter clothes were hung because the strong smell kept the moths away. *God help the moths*, she thought as she groped among the cloaks. This had been a good hiding place for them as small children, but only as long as you could hold your breath. She emerged, gasping. While she got her breath, she looked around. *Hold on a minute!* The guest room door was closed now. Uncle Hugh must have come in while she was in the garderobe. Perhaps he'd seen James from the battlements. But she wasn't going to make the mistake of barging in twice; she knocked and waited ... and waited ... No reply. She called his name. Still no reply. She turned to go, then, unmistakably, heard a board creak. Careful not to make a noise, she tiptoed back to the door, raised the latch, and pushed it open. There was her tutor, Dr Fenton, bent over the table, leafing through Uncle Hugh's papers. She cleared her throat. He looked up with what could only be described as a guilty start.

'Oh Sinéad, my dear. You startled me! I'm just doing a little tidying up for the Earl. By the way, your Father's back if you want to talk to him.'

She stood confused, he sounded so normal. But why ... *why didn't he answer my knock? Why didn't he say something when I called out?* The answer hit her like a blow between the eyes: he *wasn't* tidying things up for Uncle Hugh, he was *spying* on him, going through his papers! He had thought she would go away, but she hadn't, had she? *We were right – me and Fion!* Fury boiled inside her. *I'll confront him, watch him squirm like the worm he is. But no, wait a moment;* she knew grown-ups, he would just deny it, say she was lying. People always listened to grown-ups. She managed to give him a wan smile and backed away, closing the door after her. *Keep calm, Sinéad. Think! I must find Uncle Hugh before Fenton thinks I'm suspicious of him. If Uncle Hugh catches him, that will clinch matters once and for all. Oh please God Uncle Hugh's still on the battlements!* She walked slowly to the spiral staircase and then flew up the stone steps. There, miraculously, was Uncle Hugh, at the self-same spot where they had stood earlier. He turned as she ran up.

'Steady, child! Don't throw yourself over. Well, what have you got for me now? Harmony and light among my young warriors?'

'It's Dr Fenton!' she gasped. 'Fion suggested it because of the worm in my apple; he took his dagger to it ...' Words poured out of her; there seemed to be so many threads to tie together.

'Stop, child – stop! Take a big breath and get to the nub of the matter.'

Sinéad took a gulp of air and started again. 'Remember your rotten apple? Well, Fion and I think that someone in the castle has been getting at James, trying to make him go over to the English side. We suspected our tutor, Dr Fenton, but we had no proof. Now I have proof. Dr Fenton is a spy!'

'Fenton! I find that hard to believe. "Spy" is a strong word, Sinéad. What's your proof?'

'Did you ask Dr Fenton to help you sort out the papers in your room?'

'No!' A look of thunder gathered on the Earl's face. 'By God, no!' His hand flew to his breast pocket from which he drew out a sheaf of papers, neatly folded. 'Never say that I am not careful, Sinéad. They're all here – my plans are safe!' He expelled a blast of air. 'So, Henry Fenton's our rotten apple. As your father's secretary he must have known that I was coming here. It wouldn't surprise me if he's managed to get word out to Chichester. We may have visitors. I must get ready to leave. This is the story of my life now,' he said angrily. He thumped the battlements with his fist. 'Damn young Con! Why does he have to go missing today of all days?' He saw consternation on Sinéad's face. 'Don't mistake me. I love that boy like no other, but just now I could wring his neck.'

Sinéad looked out over the battlements and stiffened. 'Perhaps you will be able to, Uncle.'

'What do you mean?'

'Look there! Nobody here can ride like that. Here he comes!'

And there, indeed, came Con, lying low along his pony's back, his legs thrashing at Macha's sides like small wings. From up there, pony and boy looked like a bird sweeping low across the ground towards them.

'Come on, Con!' roared Hugh, thumping Sinéad on the back. 'Come on!'

She looked up at Uncle Hugh and laughed; he was a different man already. Gone was the elderly stoop as he urged his son on. 'I smell trouble, Sinéad, and I'd better get down and see what that young rascal has to say for himself. He may be a little divil, but it strikes me that it could well be that the real devil is after him. We'll elope some other time, my dear.' And with that he was off down the steps with the speed and agility of a goat.

Sinéad ran down so fast after him that her skirts filled with air and she felt as light as thistledown, but she missed her footing at the bottom and completed the last four steps on her behind. But she was on her feet in a second and out the door just in time to see young Con ride up to the foot of the ramp below the door where his father was waiting.

'Con O'Neill, where the hell have you been? Come down off that pony while I skelp you!' Two brawny arms reached up for the lad, who pitched himself readily enough into them. What followed was more of a hug than a skelping, though it was followed by a sharp smack on the backside as Hugh put the lad down. Sinéad joined them; she couldn't wait to meet Con.

'Father! Chichester's coming!' Con said, panting.

'I *thought* you had a devil after you. D'you hear that, Sinéad? That's how to give a message, no beating about the bush.' He turned to Con. 'So, how long do we have? Are they hot on your heels?'

Con shook his head. 'No, sir. I took a short cut over the hill. I got lost. But they're on foot, mostly. Maybe an hour if they wait for the foot soldiers.'

'How many horsemen, son?'

'Six, sir. And Sir Chichester, of course.'

'They won't ride ahead, not with just six; they'll stay with the foot soldiers. Did you count how many on foot?'

'I tried. I think there were about seventy in all. Musket men–'

But Hugh interrupted. 'Details will do later, son. Well done!' He turned to Sinéad. 'Hear that, Sinéad? Con says Chichester is coming. We must leave immediately. Go tell your father.'

'But can't you stay? We can protect you, surely.'

'No arguing! All I've got to lose is my head, but your father has his lands and his castle, not to mention you and his family to think of. The sooner I'm out of here the better. Just go, and go quickly, but take the boy and see that he gets a bite to eat.'

Having found Father and given him her message, she took Con out to the kitchens and fed him till she thought he would burst. It was a spluttery affair, as his need to tell his story was about as urgent as his need to eat. He had her alternately on the edge of her seat, and then laughing out loud. No doubt, he would tell the story many times in the future, but this was his first opportunity and he made the most of it. She was intrigued by the man who had helped him. Who was this 'Haystacks' who spoke like a poet and just seemed to spring up out of the ground?

As they came out of the kitchen she remembered that she had still not located James. On a previous visit, Uncle Hugh had taught her how to wolf-whistle. If nothing else would carry to

James over the present preparations, a wolf-whistle would. She gave a long, sharp, ear-splitting blast.

When she looked down, she found Con gazing at her in open-mouthed awe. His voice was almost a whisper: 'Oh do show me how to do that!'

So she did.

CHAPTER 8

Preparing for the Enemy

t was as if a hurricane had hit the castle. Father was up, washed, dressed, and giving orders. The broken old soldier sitting hunched over his stick was gone; now he stood and pointed with the stick, like a general in the field. Servants were moving the screens that concealed his retreat at the end of the great hall. Dr Fenton was working furiously, putting papers into chests, while Father questioned Uncle Hugh about his plans. Sinéad hovered in the background, wanting to be in on it all.

'The kitchens will have food for your party ready in a quarter of an hour, Hugh,' said Father. 'How many are you?'

'We'll be six. On horses will be myself, Con, and, if you will release him, Fion; the rest on foot.'

'Must you take Fion? He's a great favourite here and James'll miss him.'

Sinéad glanced at Uncle Hugh. Would he mention the duel? 'Yes, and I'm sure he'll miss James in turn. But one of Chichester's

77

favourite ploys is to take hostages, and after seeing young Red Hugh when he'd escaped from Dublin Castle, I won't give Chichester the pleasure taking any nephew of mine as a hostage, if I can prevent it.'

'How on earth did Chichester come to know you were here?'

'Oh, I've learned long ago that even stones have ears.'

Sinéad didn't turn to where Dr Fenton was working, but she listened. The hasty packing of documents had stopped ... now it started again. She looked at Uncle Hugh, who glanced in her direction – was that the shade of a wink? Obviously, he couldn't talk to Father while Fenton was listening. Uncle Hugh went on: 'I haven't seen Fion to tell him we're going; perhaps Sinéad knows where he is?'

'I'll go and find him,' she said, and slipped quickly out of the room. As she left, she heard Father say: 'I've decided to greet Chichester as a guest. He's as prickly as a hedgehog and I don't want to give him any cause to try to turn us off our lands. He's not forgiven my friendship with you despite our pardon; I want to show that I've got nothing to hide.'

'Apart from me, my old friend. I must indeed be gone!'

<hr />

As Sinéad ran to the falconry, she realised that the flurry of activity had spread out here too. The armourer had his furnace glowing white, as men queued for hurried repairs to metal buckles, to pike shafts, to sword hilts. A boy was turning a great circular grind-stone, as soldiers lined up to sharpen their pikes and swords; fountains of sparks burst from the spinning stone.

'Hey! ... Fion?' she called from among the bird perches, eyeing the ceiling above. 'It's me ... Sinéad. Can I come up?'

Fion's voice came from above. 'Is James around? And what in heaven's name is happening?'

'I don't know where James is,' she called. 'He's disappeared. But Chichester's about to arrive with a whole army.'

'Holy smoke! So they got word out to him!' There was a scuffle of movement above, and dust and fragments rained down. Sinéad backed away as Fion emerged from the loft and dropped to the ground.

'It's not "they", Fion, I'm sure of it now, but we were right about Fenton. I found him poking in Uncle Hugh's papers pretending he was sorting them. You ought to have seen Uncle Hugh's face when I told him.'

'Mark my words, they're in it together. Why was James needling me all morning, going on at me, provoking me to fight that stupid duel? Of course he knew! I'd be a nice mouse to lay at Chichester's feet, neatly skewered. I bet you anything you like that James is out there now showing Chichester the way. Just think of the reward: "Hugh O'Neill dead or alive – £50". That's the rumour.'

'Oh shut up, Fion,' she snapped. 'It's nothing to do with James. He would never betray a guest under his own roof, let alone betray him for gold!'

'Humph. So how do we know the Lord Deputy's coming?'

'Con's back. He was captured by them, but escaped and found a way through the plashing to warn us. You're leaving now with Uncle Hugh ... and you're wrong about James, I'm sure of it.' *But where is he?* she worried.

Fion cocked his head at the clanging from the armoury. 'So are you getting ready to fight the English, then?'

'No. Father's planning to greet Sir Chichester as a guest. With Uncle Hugh gone, you see, we'll have nothing to hide.'

'So I'm to go too? I'd like to have seen the old terror for myself!'

'No, you must go. Uncle Hugh says Chichester will be looking for hostages.'

'Perhaps he'll take brother James, then!' he said snidely.

Sinéad winced.

Fion climbed up into his loft and appeared a minute or two later with two saddlebags, which he lowered down to her.

❦

Twenty minutes later Uncle Hugh's small party of six set off into the woods behind the castle. Farewells had been brief. Con pleaded to be allowed to stay for the battle.

'Thanks to you, Con, there won't be a battle,' laughed Uncle Hugh.

Sinéad was there to wave them off. As Fion passed, he bent down. 'I'm sorry it's ending like this, Sinéad. I have no quarrel with you.' He touched his pony's flanks, and was gone.

Sinéad's hand dropped to her side. She felt a void open in her life.

Sinéad had little interest in the frenetic activity in the castle. If they weren't preparing for war, what was all the fuss about? She was sad at the departure of Uncle Hugh, and at the way Fion had said goodbye as if he would never see her again. When she was hauled away by her mother to get dressed, it seemed like treachery to put on Uncle Hugh's beautiful dress to greet his worst enemy.

'But Mother, Con says he's like the devil himself ...' but the rest of her sentence was lost as her Mother, aided by Kathleen, lowered Uncle Hugh's fabulous dress over her head. She emerged pink and furious. 'I should be wearing armour, not this ... this meringue!'

Mother seemed to be about to give her a slap, but then changed her mind. Sounding as if she was addressing a five-year-old, she explained: 'Now listen, Sinéad. We have just learned that the Lord Deputy of Ireland, Sir Arthur Chichester, is about to make a courtesy call on the King of England's loyal subject, Sir Malachy de Cashel–'

'Why are you talking like that? If you mean Father, say *Father*, and you know perfectly well he's not loyal to that old goat, the king – ouch!' She received a stinging slap on the leg.

'Sinéad, will you stop being foolish! This may seem like a game, but one wrong word and you could ruin everything. Listen now: Father *is* loyal! He *was* pardoned by the King, just like Uncle Hugh, after the battle of Kinsale, and neither of them has taken up arms against King James since then.'

'Then why is Uncle Hugh on the run?' said Sinéad, sullenly.

'Because Chichester hates him, and wants to send him to England where the King will either behead him or lock him up in the Tower of London. By entertaining Sir Arthur and his troops, we are giving Uncle Hugh time to escape. We will also be showing our loyalty to the Crown so that Chichester will have no reason to confiscate our lands and give them to some English planter. Be polite to them, show respect and the manners that Dr Fenton has taught you.'

The thought of Uncle Hugh – *her* Uncle Hugh – being beheaded finally sobered Sinéad. Tears pricked in her eyes. 'So, what do we say about Uncle Hugh, and Con?'

'If anyone asks you about either of them, just look stupid, like you were just now!'

Sinéad, feeling sad and a little ashamed, made a face. Mother gave her a kiss. 'There's no need for Chichester to know anything about our visitors, my dear.' Sinéad nodded, but then suddenly sat up, alert. This was nonsense! Chichester would be told everything as soon as he was in the door.

'But Fenton, Mother!'

'What do you mean, "Fenton?" You mustn't speak about him like that; have some respect, girl. He's Dr Fenton!'

In that instant Sinéad realised that Mother didn't know about him. *Holy smoke, does that mean that Father doesn't know either? What if Uncle Hugh hasn't had time to tell him?* It had all been so rushed.

'Let me go, Mother! I must speak to Father!' She ran for the door.

'Stop, child! You're open down the back!' Kathleen grabbed her, and Sinéad stood trembling with impatience as the maid struggled with the line of tiny buttons and loops down her spine. *Oh get on, Kathleen!* she thought.

When she burst into the great hall she found a queue of people waiting for Father's instructions. Fenton was there, hovering around him like an over-willing spaniel. How could she find out if Father knew that Fenton was a spy without blurting it out in front of the scoundrel?

At that moment, Father caught sight of her, waiting. He looked surprised. 'My word, child, you *are* dressed up. Are you looking for me?'

She'd forgotten about the dress. His surprise threw her for a moment, and now Fenton's protruding eyes were fixed on her. Would Uncle Hugh have mentioned apples, rotten apples per-haps? It was worth a try.

'Father, did ... did Uncle Hugh tell you what we found in the apples? He said it might be important.' She watched her father's face ... a moment of puzzlement, then it cleared.

'He did tell me, love. I'm going to deal with it later. It's codling-moth, you know.'

She nearly danced with excitement. *He's got it, he's got it!*

But the victualler was patting her on the head. 'This is not the moment to bother your father with moths, dear! Run along, now!'

She stepped back into the shadows, happy that Father knew. She listened to his crisp orders – no wonder Uncle Hugh had wanted Father beside him at Kinsale. Now he was detailing exactly how many horsemen and men-at-arms were to make up the party that would go out to greet the Lord Deputy. Next he turned to the chief herdsman. All but a small herd of cattle were to be moved out of sight into the woods; however, a fat bullock was to be slaughtered straight away and pit-roasted for the common soldiers. 'Yes, yes,' he instructed, 'all that's necessary for seventy men.'

'So we know their number, Milord?' asked the victualler, who had re-joined the line.

'Yes, thanks to our informant, we even know the colour of their eyes,' joked Father. 'A good spy is worth a thousand men, eh Fenton?' His secretary smiled weakly. Father's instructions flowed on: 'We will be entertaining the Deputy and six gentlemen. The high table will be me and six members of the household, including Dr Fenton here.'

At that moment Sinéad felt a hand on her shoulder and heard a whisper in her ear. 'For God's sake, Sinéad, what's going on?'

She turned in surprise. It was James, smudged and covered in cobwebs. She grabbed him by the elbow and hurried him out of the hurly burly of the castle to an angle of the wall where they could talk privately.

'Well, James, *you* tell *me* what it's all about!' she demanded.

'I've no idea; I was ... far away and didn't hear anything till now.'

'Rot! You'd have had to be in France to miss the commotion here! Look at you, you're covered in cobwebs!' She brushed at him, but he slapped her hand away.

'I have a hiding place ... a deep place ... I didn't hear anything,' he said sullenly.

Sinéad was still suspicious of his involvement. 'Chichester's coming here to catch Uncle Hugh,' she informed her brother. 'We thought you might be with him.'

'Me! With Uncle Hugh? No way!'

'No, you oaf. With Chichester, the Lord Deputy. We thought you'd gone over to the other side.'

'We ...who's *we*? Fion, I bet! Well, of all the bloody cheek! Anyway, how could Chichester know that Uncle Hugh's here?'

'Because someone told him!'

'You mean a *spy*?'

'Yes, we thought ...' Just then a bellow rang out from the castle door above them: 'Master James to Sir Malachy immediately!'

James sprang to his feet but Sinéad caught him and held on. 'You can't go in like that, covered in cobwebs!' She began to brush his jacket and pluck strands from his hair. 'And look, your face is all smudged!' she said, pulling a kerchief from her sleeve.

'Hey!' he protested. 'I don't want my face washed in your spit!'

'Well, use your own spit then!' she said, holding out the hand-kerchief. While he scrubbed at his face and hands she told him how the alarm had been given by young Con, and how Uncle Hugh had left, taking Fion with him.

'Good-riddance! I've had enough of Fion and Uncle Hugh, and the native Irish forever.'

Sinéad bit her tongue. He hadn't known about Chichester, that was the important thing, so he hadn't been in on Fenton's plot. 'Father plans to treat Sir Chichester as a guest. That's what he's arranging now.'

'Good! Dr Fenton says we should treat the English in Ireland as our guests, not our enemies. If we honour them, they will honour us.' He pushed her away. 'I must go!'

'James, there's something else you must know. It's about Fenton–' but he was gone.

Greensleeves

As James ran up the ramp into the castle and thrust himself into the throng in the great hall, he was grateful for his clean-up, and also for Sinéad's briefing about what was going on. Willing hands pushed him forward to where Father sat in his ornate chair.

Dr Fenton, who hadn't noticed James's arrival, was pleading with Father. 'Sir, I think it would be more appropriate for me, as your secretary, to greet the Lord Deputy. Your son–' but Father had seen James arrive, and brushed his secretary aside. 'About time too, James! Where have you been?' He didn't wait for an answer. 'I am unable to ride out to greet the Lord Deputy and I am trying to persuade Dr Fenton here that it is appropriate that you, as my son and heir, should ride out and greet our guest.'

James was thrilled. He glanced at his tutor, who apparently was having a change of heart: 'Of course, of course, Sir Malachy ... most appropriate.'

James felt magnanimous. *Good old Fenton. And I am prepared. It's an honour, and it's time we Irish Normans met the English as equals.* He straightened his shoulders. 'Sir, I would be honoured,' he said with a bow.

'Well, go and make yourself respectable, and come back to me immediately for instructions.'

At least Kathleen gave him water to wash in. Then she stood back and eyed him up and down. He tried to imagine how he looked. Father's riding boots with their floppy, turned-down tops fitted well enough with several extra pairs of socks inside. Then he had a pair of hose meeting maroon-coloured pantaloons, which spread out over his thighs in generous puffs. A clean linen shirt, a rust-coloured doublet, and a broad-brimmed hat, to which Kathleen had hastily sewn some sweeping feathers, completed his outfit.

'You can doff that hat like a real gentleman, so you can,' she said. James tried to look superior; *but I am a real gentleman*, then he cringed as Kathleen added: 'You're just gorgeous, you are!' He clattered down the stairs to present himself to Father for final instructions.

'You will have the captain of the guard with you. Do as he says, but above all be polite. You know – and they know – that they are not invited, but by greeting them civilly, we can at least preserve our dignity.' Father looked grim. 'You may be sure there will be a price to pay. Chichester expects to find Hugh O'Neill here, and will be furious when he's not, but remember, Uncle Hugh is the rightful Earl of Tyrone. We have done nothing illegal!' At that, he handed James his sword, the sharp one that had been denied him that morning. James almost felt as if he'd been knighted as he buckled it on proudly. 'Dr Fenton will advise you on how to address the Lord Deputy.'

James could hear the rat-ta-ta-tat of the drum before the army emerged from the forest road. As he rode out, the captain explained to him how they would present themselves to the advancing force. 'Remember, Master James, that we've come to welcome them, not attack them. Thanks to young O'Neill, we know exactly how many cavalry Sir Arthur has with him, so we match them horse for horse. At the same time we want to keep them together and not have them galloping off around the place, searching for the Earl, or indeed going chasing after him. He's only an hour ahead of them, after all. I have arranged for archers and some extra horse to remain out of sight along the forest edge with orders to show themselves only if necessary.'

James was grateful for the flow of talk as the captain went on to say: 'What you have to do is to act the young gentleman that you are, and they will behave like gentlemen — for the moment anyway. If they don't, we'll be right behind you.' James's mouth was dry. Just now all he wanted to do was turn around and gallop back to the safety of the castle, but the captain leant across and clapped him on the shoulder. 'You'll be just fine. Ride on, now, about twenty paces ahead so they know you are a spokesman, and remember to reach for your hat, not your sword.' There was a low murmur of encouragement from the common soldiers behind him as James rode forward by himself. He mustn't let them down.

The small army came into sight, a solid phalanx of marching men, the sunlight glittering on their armour and their swaying pikes. The drum rattled, and a low cloud of dust rose waist deep about them. At their head rode a single horseman, his face concealed in the shadow of his visor. Further horsemen, wearing bright cloaks and broad-brimmed hats, rode loosely on each side of the column. When they saw the castle ahead, they began to urge their horses forward, spreading out on each side, but a barked order from their leader brought them back to the column. One of them, however, seemed to have lost control of his horse and to be intent on charging into the forest, head-on. Two archers stepped silently from the trees, with arrows notched; the man's horse shied. For a moment it looked as if he would fall off, but one of the archers obligingly caught the horse's reins, calmed it, and led it back towards the marching men.

'Dwatted horse!' James heard the rider curse, as the archer released it.

He could see the face of the leader now, his beard jutting out over his breastplate; he did not seem amused at the incident. So, this must be Sir Arthur Chichester, the most powerful man in Ireland. But Fenton had assured him that he was just waiting to welcome families like James's back into the English fold: 'Remember, James, they are gentlemen – harsh, cruel perhaps, but just and true.'

James straightened his back; this was his moment. Rehearsing his greeting in English, he rode forward and reached for his hat. The general, seeing his advance, raised his right hand; behind him a sergeant bellowed 'Halt!' and the marching men stopped as one. The drum rolled, then stopped, and the dust drifted away.

When James was a horse's length from the general, he swept his hat from his head and with a deep bow said, 'My Lord Chichester, Lord Deputy of Ireland, on behalf of my father, Sir Malachy de Cashel, I bid you welcome to our castle and to our demesne.'

'Where is your father, boy?'

'He sends his apologies; he is at present unable to ride.'

'A bullet in the leg at Kinsale, if my memory serves me, fighting on the wrong side.'

'We have Our Gracious Majesty, King James's pardon, my Lord, and are looking forward to greeting you in the castle.'

'*Our* Gracious Majesty, indeed.' James felt the general's eyes boring into him. 'Are you the lad that Henry Fenton is tutoring?'

'Yes, sir, Dr Fenton is indeed my tutor.' *How can someone like Sir Arthur Chichester know about Fenton and me? Does he know everything?* But Father had said: Leave his questions to me. James bowed.

'May I take you to my father, sir? Perhaps we can provide you with some refreshment?' As he wheeled his horse around by way of invitation, he thought of the turmoil in the kitchens – the ox, and the barrels of wine fresh broached in the undercroft. Sir Arthur raised his hand, the sergeant barked, the drum beat, and James felt as if he himself was the general riding ahead of the army.

'You seem to be prepared for my coming, lad. What is your name?' asked Sir Arthur.

'James, sir. Your fame goes before you, sir.' James had just thought of this compliment and was rather pleased with it.

He was rewarded with a grunt. 'You speak English, boy, but you have the slippery tongue of the Irish.' James blushed to the roots of his hair. *Don't try to be too clever, you fool!* he told himself, but Chichester went on: 'There's a young lad, rides a pony – yellow shirt, red hair – have you seen him?'

James recognised Sinéad's description of young Con at once, but he himself hadn't seen Con so he could say without a blush, 'No, sir, there's no one like that here.' The eyes that glinted from under the general's visor forced him to look away. Thank God they were now approaching the castle where he could busy himself calling for grooms for their horses, while his own captain invited the English sergeant to dismiss his men and bring them over to where the roasting ox was already emitting inviting smells. James dismounted, and, carrying his hat, led the English general and his fellow officers up the ramp and into the great hall of the castle. He hardly recognised it. Torches blazed from the sconces about the walls, and the floor was freshly strewn with rushes. Seated under the canopy that shaded his great oak chair sat Father.

James led the visitors forward, and, as rehearsed with Dr Fenton, announced: 'Sir Malachy de Cashel, may I present Sir Arthur Chichester, Lord Deputy of Ireland.'

The general, who had removed his helmet, came forward, and with a stiff bow, greeted Father. He then introduced his lieutenants who, in turn, stepped forward, bowing and sweeping their plumed hats low in front of them. Foremost of these, to James's surprise, was the officer whose horse had bolted for the forest.

'Sir Geoffrey Bonmann!' growled the general.

'Sir Geoffwey, at your service,' the man said with an elaborate bow. James had to suppress a smile.

The company was then released to make free of the castle while final preparations for dinner were made.

The roar and clatter of conversation, the reek of smoke from the torches, and the hurried steps of servants serving the top table, was as heady as the wine and ale that was liberally served. The banquet was well advanced, and James had hardly had a bite, partly out of excitement, but partly because Father had called on him to act as his squire.

'James,' he would say, leaning back to where James was standing behind him, 'Sir Arthur's glass!' and James would take a jug from one of the servants and see that the great man's glass was topped up; then he would see to the glasses of the other guests at the top table. Of them all, Chichester drank the least. The seating had been arranged by Fenton, who seemed, in some mysterious way, to know where everyone should sit according to their rank. 'Dr Fenton knows about these things,' Father had said with a mysterious chuckle. James picked up snatches of conversation: at one minute Chichester was asking Father about his harvest, and then next was turning to Mother to tell her of changes in fashion in London since Elizabeth, the old queen, had died. Not a word about past battles, not a word about Hugh O'Neill. It was all just as Fenton had said it would be – fine words and good manners.

Outside, the common soldiers were happily eating their way through their roasted ox. Inside the castle, however, the meats on offer were just the finer cuts.

'I'm sorry the beef's so fresh, Sir Arthur,' Father shouted over the swell of voices. 'If we'd known you were coming we'd have had it hanging for you this past week.' Then, beckoning to James, 'What else do we have to offer, son?'

'We have venison – that's really ripe, sir – then there's pork, and, of course, mutton; and I believe a suckling pig is on its way. We have fowl too, if you'd prefer a lighter meat.'

'I'll stick with the beef. As an old campaigner, Sir Malachy, I've found that most meats cooked within an hour or so of slaughter eat remarkably well.'

James called to the servers to bring beef. 'Fillet for Sir Arthur!'

At the high table they ate off silver plates, while 'below the salt' the meat was served on bread trenchers. James's mouth watered; he preferred a trencher any time – 'loved by boys and dogs' grown-ups would laugh. The delicious gravy would soak into the bread to be eaten last or thrown to the dogs.

What's Sir Arthur saying to Mother? He leaned forward. 'Your daughter is quite a charmer, madam, and dressed in the height of fashion, I see.' James followed his gaze to where he could see Sinéad in animated conversation with two of their visitors. He'd not had time to appreciate her new dress. In this setting, the transformation took him by surprise. He'd never thought of his sister as pretty, let alone a charmer, but just now she did look – well – quite stunning he supposed, and very grown-up. Sir Arthur was chuckling. 'She seems to have caught young Bonmann's eye.'

'Ah, she's only a child! But he'll regret it – she'd talk the legs off a donkey!' smiled Mother.

'She might be doing just that,' said Sir Arthur, with a small, tight smile. As if Sinéad had become aware of the eyes on her from the high table she blushed and got up to leave the room.

Father turned to James. 'Go, boy, get yourself something to eat,' and James went off willingly enough; he was starving. He couldn't see Sinéad, but he did notice that the officer called Bonmann was making his way after her towards the door. His own priority now was food.

Up to this moment, Sinéad had loved the plumed hats, the silk doublets and coloured hose of the men, the colours all varied in the ruddy glow of the torches on the walls and the yellow glow from the candelabras on the tables. She had been frightened for James when he had ridden out to meet the army, but they seemed friendly; she had imagined something much more formidable. Now Father had cleverly turned the incident into a party, and she was loving it. Perhaps James was right and the English didn't all have horns and tails. For the first time in her life, she found herself the centre of attention among a group of men who were treating her as if she really were a young lady, not just a child in a pretty dress. She responded by simply being herself, answering their questions and laughing at their jokes, most of which she didn't really understand. They were like children themselves; when she admired their plumed hats and embroidered doublets, they would blush and preen like peacocks. Rather tactlessly, she told how they had once had a peacock that had been eaten by their wolfhound! They complimented her on her English, laughing when she slipped in an Irish word by mistake.

There was one of them she didn't like, however, as he had an irritating habit of touching her as he spoke – her hair, her cheek, her shoulder. His said her English was 'Wemarkable'. As she didn't understand the word, she queried it: 'Wemarkable?' she asked. And for some reason this caused a gale of laughter from all the others. That was the moment that she noticed the people at the high table looking in her direction and decided that perhaps she should leave. There were screens along the walls so the servants could come and go without disturbing the feast, so she ducked behind these and moved towards the door. Then, suddenly, her way was blocked. It was the young man with the funny way of speaking. *Bonham, that's his name,* she remembered. *Perhaps he's looking for the garderobe?*

'Over there,' she said, pointing towards the opposite corner, and moved to pass him, but as if by accident he stepped in her way. They both laughed, she nervously. She tried again, and this time it was no accident. He was deliberately blocking her way. Quite suddenly she just wanted to get away from him. There was a gap between the screens, so she squeezed through, back into the banquet area, and made for the castle door, where she breathed in great gulps of the clean night air. The camp-fires of the visiting army glowed and sparked. There were shouts, followed by gales of laughter; occasionally a voice would be raised, but it seemed no wilder than on a normal holiday night. At least her heart had stopped thumping ... At that moment an arm was laid over her shoulders and she froze.

'No place for a pwetty little girl like you!'

She tried to move away. His hand tightened on her shoulder.

'Don't wiggle, my sweetheart.'

Sweetheart! That was a word she hated. 'Your men seem to be enjoying themselves,' she said. *Oh, how can I get away?* she thought.

'Not as much as I am enjoying you, my sweetheart.'

She elbowed herself around in a fury, thinking, *I'm nobody's sweetheart!* – and she moved to walk past him, but he put his hand under her chin, and forced her to look up. Now his face was looming closer and closer – his wet lips – she wrenched her face to one side, as his meagre moustache brushed her cheek.

Then, from just behind her, came a voice: 'Are you all right, Miss Sinéad?' The rough voice of the guard was music to her ears. It startled the young man, who loosened his grip on her shoulders. She tore herself free, ducked under his arm, and fled for the stairs and the safety of her bedroom.

It was there that James found her twenty minutes later. 'What on earth are you doing up here?'

'I'm hiding from him!'

'Him?'

'That creep, Bonham.'

'It's Bonmann, not Bonham. A *bonham*'s a piglet in Irish, as you well know – and he's a gentleman! He can't be a creep! Do you know he's the son of the Earl of Middlesex, for God's sake! If he was teasing you, you deserved it. I saw you flirting with them all quite shamelessly!'

'Flirting! I wasn't flirting. It's just they started laughing over some mistake I made in English. Then, when I saw you all looking at me from the high table, I went to get some air, and he followed me. It was horrible, James. He kept touching me and even tried–'

'Oh nonsense, Sinéad. Think how Uncle Hugh tickles you and throws you around.' Sinéad thought wistfully of Uncle Hugh, how just today he'd pretended they were going to elope, but this had been quite different. James was going on, 'It's Uncle Hugh's fault anyway, dressing you up like a fast woman.'

Sinéad slapped him for that, but there was no force behind it; she didn't have the energy. 'Anyway, what are you doing up here yourself?' she asked.

'A harper's turned up. Why do we have to entertain the English with bog music?'

'Oh I love a harper! Why didn't you tell me? I wonder ...' *Could this be Con's poet?*

'What do you wonder?'

But she didn't tell him. 'Oh just mind your own business; you don't know the half of what goes on here. I'm going down, and you can be my protector.'

<hr>

They arrived back in the hall to hear a polite patter of applause as the harper finished his first piece. Sinéad cursed herself for having missed him. He was younger than she expected, a trim beard, with just a wisp of grey in the hair that was clasped behind in a ponytail. His face was dark, as someone is who spends much of his life on the road. She edged closer to him, trying to read his face. *Serious,* she thought, *but those are laughter lines about his eyes.* He was wearing the traditional poet's gown; they kept a spare one in the castle for musicians and poets of the proper rank. The hum of conversation was growing again, but he seemed lost in his own world, his hands running over the strings of the harp like two butterflies barely touching the strings. One of the visitors turned to him and asked him a question in English; he smiled and shrugged apologetically, indicating that he didn't understand English. A servant was passing with a jug of mead, so Sinéad got him a mug of the golden honey brew and carried over to him.

'Welcome to our home,' she said in Irish, and bobbed a curtsey. 'I hope you will play again because I missed your first piece.'

He looked up, and his eyes crinkled as he smiled. 'Thank you, child, I will play again. Just now I am trying to remember a tune that might please your guests. They tell me it was composed by old King Henry, though I doubt it. Talk to me while I send the music down to my fingers.' So Sinéad told him who she was and who made up the gathering. 'Thank you, my dear,' he said. 'I had a dream about a boy on a horse in a saffron shirt. Do you ever have dreams like that?'

Sinéad laughed. 'That's strange because I too had just such a dream and he was talking, of all things, to a haystack!' She dropped her voice. 'He came in time to see his father and his party safely away. He would wish you well.'

The harper nodded. 'The tune I was searching for seems to have reached my fingers now, so let's see if they recognise it.' Then, without any apparent change in volume, the harp began to fill the room with a pure and enchanting melody. The roar of voices fell to a hum, then a murmur. Sinéad sat back happily. Compared to Irish airs it was simple, a melody that invited a song. The visitors were smiling, recognising it and swaying to it. Then, out of the murk of the smoky room, a single voice rose, singing in a light tenor:

Alas, my love, you do me wrong,

To cast me off discourteously.

And I have lov-ed you so long,

Delighting in your companie.

Greensleeves was all my joy

Greensleeves was my delight,

Greensleeves was my heart of gold,

And who but my Ladie Greensleeves.

She sat back with her eyes closed, suspended between the rippling flow of the harp and the clear voice of the singer. There were many verses.

Thy cwimson stockings all of silk ...

What! Sinéad sat up, startled: *Cwimson?* It couldn't be ...

Thy girdle of gold so wed ...

Red, not wed! she nearly shouted. Her eyes opened and there he was, coming towards her, gazing at her with that watery expression she hated. How could God have given such a perfect voice to a creep like that? It was more than she could bear. In a second she was on her feet and blundering for the door, first to sniggers, then to cheers as she thrust the guard at the door to one side and fled up stairs to ... to throw herself over the battlements ... indeed, why not?

CHAPTER 10

Penalties and a Proposal

ames woke the following morning to a feeling of unease. Sir Arthur had spoken to him roughly the night before: 'Tell your Father I want the officers of the household assembled in your great hall at seven without fail.' James had hesitated – surely it was for Father to issue orders in his own castle? But the general had snapped: 'Don't just stand there, boy. Go!' The incident had been turning over in his mind, keeping him awake. Now he had overslept.

His next shock came when he entered the great hall and saw pikemen – English pikemen – lining the walls. *I suppose Father's asked them in*, he wondered as he stretched to see over the heads of the assembly to Father's seat at the top of the table. There, to his astonishment, sitting in Father's chair, under Father's canopy, was Sir Arthur Chichester.

He felt Sinéad's hand on his elbow. 'How dare he!' she whispered, loud enough to turn a few heads. 'That's Father's chair! No one, but no one, is allowed to sit in it.' Her indignation ran as a vibration into his arm.

Then came Dr Fenton's voice close beside them. 'Oh but you're wrong, child. You see, because Sir Arthur represents King James he has precedence over everyone! But I should be at your father's side, he may need my advice,' and at that he was gone, oiling himself through the crowd.

'Look at him, he's loving this,' Sinéad hissed. 'He's all cock-a-hoop!'

James snapped back: 'Shh ... Fenton's all right. But I should be up there too.' He began to thrust himself forward. *So ... Sir Arthur represents the king; now we will see justice.* He straightened his shoulders, but still a chill ran through him.

Sir Arthur was standing now, a scroll in his hand. Gone were the courtesies and fine phrases, and his voice had a rasp to it that would have cut through stone.

'You, Sir Malachy, are called to account for the non-payment of rent and for your part in rebellion against the Crown.'

No mention of hiding Hugh O'Neill, that's a relief, thought James.

Now Sir Arthur was reading from legal documents and agreements that James couldn't pretend to understand. Several times, Fenton raised minor objections on Father's side, but these were instantly shot down. Finally Sir Arthur's voice rose to an even sharper edge.

'Here is my judgement. You, Sir Malachy de Cashel, will

provide one hundred beef cattle from your herds immediately.'

A hundred cattle! James's mind leapt in a rapid calculation: *that would ruin us!* But that was not all.

'Furthermore, due to the itinerant nature of your neighbour, Hugh O'Neill, you are required, on His Majesty's behalf, to negotiate with the said Hugh O'Neill or his tenants for the immediate supply of three hundred beef cattle, to be delivered to the Pale within a period of one month from this day.'

There was a stunned silence. Sir Arthur let the scroll snap shut in his hand. An angry murmur rose from the castle people gathered in the hall. The English officers moved closer to Sir Arthur; experienced swordsmen all, they were an effective bodyguard. The pike men lining the walls, who had been standing at ease, now half-lowered their pikes to stand at the ready. If there was any trouble, the entire household would be surrounded by a stickle of steel.

That's not fair and *why us?* thought James, as he watched Father step forward, wincing with pain from his wound.

Father stood square and firm in front of the English general, his voice filling the room as it had rung out over more than one battlefield, and James felt pride swelling inside him.

'In acknowledgement of King James's pardon, I accept the fine of one hundred beef cattle. It will take some weeks to gather the number you demand, but they will be delivered to you in person within the month. With respect to rents and demands against Sir Hugh O'Neill, I have no authority to volunteer cattle from his tenants.'

'Then, Sir Malachy, I suggest you go back to the habits of your former allies and acquire the cattle involuntarily.'

There was another stunned silence. Sinéad pinched James's arm. 'He means steal them, James,' she whispered, 'just to turn Uncle Hugh against us. It's divide and rule – turn friends against each other. He doesn't want the beef; he just wants war between us!'

Father was speaking. 'I am no longer able to ride in active service, nor am I prepared to become a cattle raider, under any man's orders.'

Sir Arthur merely tightened his scroll; an icy smile hovered on his lips. 'In that case, Sir Malachy, I will require security. I have a fancy that your son, James, would benefit from exposure to our English ways, and I will be happy to take him as security until such time as you can supply the three hundred beeves.'

James was flabbergasted. *I served that man at table last night! Why take me? I've done nothing.* He made to step forward, but Sinéad held him back while Father spoke.

'No, sir! You cannot have my son. For all that he is only twelve years old, I need him here; I need his legs. Also, I have known grown men who have enjoyed your "hospitality" in Dublin Castle and I will not expose James, or any one of mine, to that humility.'

A murmur of supporting rage grew in the room. The armourer, who was standing beside James, put an arm like a tree trunk across his shoulders. 'Over my dead body, son,' his voice rumbled.

Then, unexpectedly, there was disturbance among Sir Arthur's entourage. Something was afoot. Plumed hats bobbed; there was an incongruous giggle. Sir Arthur glared at his officers. Then one of them went forward and whispered at length in his ear. The look of thunder changed to one of thought.

Sir Arthur turned to Sir Malachy. 'This is irregular, but I believe it is a sincere offer. One of my officers has a proposal to put to you.' He turned and announced: 'Sir Geoffrey Bonmann!'

The young officer stepped forward. 'Sir Malachy,' he began, 'duwing the time I have been your guest here, I have formed an attachment to your daughter, Jane, and ask you for her hand in mawiage. Because of her youth, I cwave your permission to take her now, and give her into to the care of my mother until she comes to be of mawiageable age. Sir Arthur is prepared to accept this awangement in lieu of taking your son as a hostage.'

There was an audible gasp throughout the hall. The armourer, now including Sinéad in his grip, squeezed her so tight that she had no air left for protest.

James's mind was in a whirl. He can't ... he mustn't ... he won't. *Sinéad hates that man! Does Father know this? Does he know Bonmann's a creep who can't even ride a horse?*

But Chichester was speaking. 'Well, Sir Malachy, what do you say? Your daughter married to a man of rank and wealth, so well connected that even I could not hang you? My price is your co-operation in bringing Hugh O'Neill to heel. Well?'

Could it be a good thing? James wondered. *Sinéad, well-married to save the whole family? Lots of girls have to marry men they don't like. She would have fine clothes, horses ...* But that was as far as he got. He looked across and saw her. He had never seen her so stricken, her face so white, so terrified that he hardly recognised it. She was staring at Father, wide-eyed. *She is my sister!* James suddenly realised, as if he had never thought about it before, and at that his sense of honour burst through.

Hardly believing his own courage, he stepped forward, and, standing as high as he could, he called out, 'Your lordship!' People stepped back to clear his view to the chair. 'As you know, I am James, the son of your host. I will go out among the tenants of Hugh O'Neill, as you command, and will bring back, by whatever means, the three hundred beef cattle you say are due to King James. In return I ask just one thing, and that is that my sister be allowed to decide for herself whom she is to marry.'

There was a mixed murmur: disapproval, surprise, admiration?

Well, I've done it! James thought. Heads turned towards Father, who was looking at his son as if he had never seen him before. However, his reply wasn't quite what James expected.

'Your Lordship,' said Sir Malachy, 'I honour the proposal made by Sir Geoffrey Bonmann for my daughter's hand in marriage, but I require that she be allowed to remain with her mother here in the castle until she is of marriageable age. With regard to the cattle due to you from Hugh O'Neill, my son is too young and inexperienced to lead the expedition he has just proposed, but I personally undertake to obtain the number of beasts you demand and will deliver them to you before autumn is advanced.'

For a moment it looked as if Chichester would reject Father's proposal, but then, gathering his dignity, he said, 'Agreed', and he turned as if to go.

But Father had raised his hand. 'One moment, your lordship. One of my household is leaving my employ and I would be grateful if you could see him safely back inside the Pale.'

'Well, he'd better be quick then!' and barking out the order for his march, Chichester led his men from the room.

What was that about? wondered James as the room cleared.

Then Father turned to Dr Fenton, who was busily gathering papers together. 'Dr Fenton, your master is waiting.' Dr Fenton's jaw dropped. 'No need to look surprised!' Father said. 'I have ample evidence of your spying for the Lord Deputy, but as you have given me and my children good service, I am paying your wages, as agreed.' He handed Dr Fenton a plump purse. 'I will send your books after you, but go! Go, before I think of your treachery again.'

Dr Fenton passed James without raising his eyes. James's hand rose as if to delay him, but then he dropped it. *So ... Sinéad was right.* The ground seemed to crumble beneath James's feet.

'Have they gone?' Sinéad asked. 'Really gone, and without me?'

'Yes, they've gone.'

'Thank you, James, for trying.' She turned to go, but Father, who had sunk back gratefully into his own chair, cleared his throat. 'Daughter, come to me, please. We have things to discuss.'

⁓⁓⁓

In his private place in the undercroft, James went over the events of the past two days again and again. He felt nothing but scorn for Fenton, but spies are a necessary evil. When all was said and done, Chichester had been harsh, but fair – hadn't he? The real cause of their trouble was not Chichester, but Hugh O'Neill. Was Chichester sending Fenton into their castle to spy on them any worse than O'Neill planting Fion in their family?

I'll wring every beast I can out of them! he swore. He'd go and tell Sinéad of his plans.

CHAPTER 11

The Duel

inéad lifted her head from her pillow. Her eyes burned like hot coals where her tears had dried. She didn't want to see, or be seen by, anyone.

'Who is it?'

'It's your bwother.'

In one furious leap, she was out of bed and screaming through the door, 'Don't you ever – ever – ever speak like that again, James!' She hammered on it as if she was already a child-bride locked up in some castle garret. Then she opened the door.

'What's the matter?' James asked. 'He's gone, you know.'

'No, he's not. He'll be back – ask Father!'

'Father?' James queried as he sat down on the bed beside her.

'He thinks I should accept him.' A shudder convulsed her. 'Rather, that he should accept Bonmann's proposal on my behalf.' Her voice was rising with indignation. 'I'm just a piece of goods – a chattel to be traded for the going price; one hundred cattle equals one chattel.' She put her head against his shoulder.

'Cheap at the price – but he can't mean it.'

'Oh yes, he can! Sir Geoffrey – the piglet – is a son of the Earl of Middlesex who owns a whole county in England. But he's a third son, so he's been sent to Ireland to seek his fortune. I told Father I didn't like him, but Father said he might never find a better match for me. In a few years I could have a fine home, beautiful clothes, horses, hawks – you name it. So I told him I didn't give a button about houses and horses and that all I wanted was to stay at home with him and Mother.'

'Why this sudden urge to marry you off?'

'He didn't tell me at once. I had to dig it out of him, miserable bit by miserable bit. You know that grandfather was tricked into handing over our castle and all our lands to King Henry years ago?' She waved her arms in a wide sweep. 'All of this: our castle, our fields, our woods, they don't belong to us, they belong to King James now, and Chichester can take the lot away from us if he wants.'

'Surrender and re-grant,' confirmed James. 'It means we hold the lands under English law now instead of under Irish law.'

'Yes,' said Sinéad, 'but what Grandfather didn't know was that the king could take it away whenever he liked – you can't do that under Irish law. Or that Chichester could take it for the king! It's outrageous.'

'But he can only do it in the king's name.'

'He can do what he likes. You saw how he sat in Father's chair "in the king's name". But if I'm married to the piglet, he can't. You heard him say, "Even I can't hang you."'

'What did you say to Father?'

'I threw a wobbly until he said that he would always ask me before any marriage was arranged.'

'Well, that's it, you can say no.'

'But I can't!' flared Sinéad, pushing him away. 'Do you think I can refuse now that I know that all our futures here in the castle are at stake? I hate the English, I don't want to become a Protestant, and I'll never wear fine clothes again. Why, oh why did Uncle Hugh give me that stupid dress?' She began to sob. 'I just want to go back to where we were before Chichester came – just you and me and Fion and the summer ahead of us.'

'Look, Sinéad, leave Fion out of it – forget him. He's no longer one of us. He's run off to the ferns with Uncle Hugh and won't dare show his head near here again. If I can persuade Father to let me go and round up the cattle he demands from O'Neill's tenants, I'll go for your sake and for Father.'

Sinéad didn't forget Fion, but without him she and James grew closer. She looked for opportunities to show her thanks for his brave gesture.

Weeks passed, and it was all hands on board to get in the harvest. This was no time for a cattle raid. Since Dr Fenton was gone, Father used James as his secretary, but James also had to take his turn at threshing the wheat, beating the grain and the chaff off the stalks with a flail. Sinéad's job was to sweep the mixture into shallow baskets so that the women could toss it in the air where the wind would blow away the light chaff, leaving the golden wheat to fall to the ground.

'Sinéad,' he said, coming up to her between bouts of threshing, 'O'Neill isn't bothering to answer our letters. The harvest's nearly finished and it's time we went to get those cattle! I'll speak to Father tonight.'

'Well?' she asked when she saw him after dinner.

He sighed: 'You won't believe this, but Father wouldn't listen. He's sending me with a cart-load of grain to Dundalk. We've got more than we need and the price is good. Can you imagine, all that way behind four lumbering oxen! I'll die.'

When he set out next morning, Sinéad rode the first mile with him. 'At least I can wear my sword again,' he said, and he leaned from his saddle and sent a spray of yellow ragwort flying. When the road plunged into the forest, he stopped. 'You'd better go back, else *the piglet* will get you.' At least they could joke about him now.

Sinéad was stabling her pony when she realised that the castle was humming again, just like the time when Con had come in with the news of Chichester's approach. An ostler hurried in.

'What's up, Padraic, have we visitors again?' she asked.

'Not coming, miss, we're going. A cattle raid, if rumours are correct,' and he rubbed his hands together. Sinéad was stunned.

But James! she thought, *he'll miss this.* Then she stopped. *This was planned!* Father had deliberately got James out of the way, and was organising the raid in his absence. *But that's not fair! James has been looking forward to this moment for weeks! I need to know more. I'll ask the Captain of the Guard – he'll know.*

'We're going north, miss, into O'Hanlon country; a little cattle business to be settled there.'

'Can I come too?' she pleaded.

But he laughed. 'I think not, miss, there might be a bit of pushing and shoving, you see.'

She worked on him then, and got a pretty good idea of their plans. Then she made plans of her own. *When James has delivered his corn, he'll be free; the empty carts won't need an escort. If I can get word to him, he might be able to strike north and meet up with the raiders. A bit of pushing and shoving doesn't sound like danger to me. Father'll be furious, of course, but this will teach him for trying to marry me off. Now, how on earth can I get word to James?*

In the guest room she bent silently over the small table where, only few weeks before, Uncle Hugh had been writing a letter to the king of England. They kept paper, a new quill, and ink here for guests. Her pen scratched on the paper. Her writing might not be elegant, but it was clear. She read the note through, then she scattered sand on it to dry the ink, folded it, and melted a blob of sealing wax in the candle. She then used a gold coin from her treasure box, to press into the wax. The coin wasn't worth much, as people had clipped bits of gold off it until it was all angles at the edge. But James would recognise its impression at once. Then she hurried downstairs to where a trader from Dundalk was waiting. He'd agreed to take the note for her. She reckoned that, riding on horseback, he would soon overtake James's lumbering ox-cart; a small coin sealed the deal.

That night she had terrible dreams.

For James, the last plodding miles into Dundalk, and the interminable negotiations for the selling of the corn had been an agony. He had read and re-read Sinéad's note. *The raid's happening, and I'm not there!* But would he be able to find the raiding party? *If I'm not quick, it'll be over!* Eventually he was able to send the empty cart on its way home, together with the lame excuse that he was going to visit relatives in town.

Many hours later, saddle-sore and weary, James sat on his pony at a crossroads. *Which way do I turn?* He could feel the heat radiating from his poor pony. Had he ridden it too hard? He tapped his shirt where Sinéad's note rustled reassuringly; he knew it by heart now. She had managed to get a lot of information from the captain of the expedition. *I'm sure this is their route, but are they ahead of me or behind?* Peasants along his road had been helpful, seeing him as a young lad who had got separated from his companions. He had kept his sword out of sight, wrapped in his cloak, but none of them had seen a party like he described coming from the south. There was, however, a rumour of a large herd of cattle gathered to the north. *Could they have got ahead of me and finished the job without me?* he worried. But the light was going, his pony was tired, and the crossroads did not feel like a safe place to linger. There were plenty of wild men who had taken to the woods when their masters had been turned off their lands, who would happily relieve him of his pony and his fine clothes, even his life.

There was just enough light for him to strike off the road and find a thicket that would give both him and his pony shelter and cover. After rubbing the pony down and giving it a nosebag of wheat he had saved from the ox-cart, he leaned against a tree. He wouldn't risk a fire, so he wrapped his cloak about him and settled down to watch the pale glimmer that showed the road from the south. He'd never been on his own like this before, Fion had always been with him on his adventures. Night-time rustles became footsteps creeping up on him; even the thumping of his heart became the thud of hooves. His head dropped forward, then jerked up – then gradually sank forward again into sleep.

<hr>

'Who is he?' said a voice. James woke with a start, pushing frantically at the cloak that had fallen over his face. He stared into a blind of light. 'Well, I'll be damned if it isn't the young master.'

'How did you find me?' he asked as he struggled to his feet, brushing off leaves and twigs from the forest floor.

'Wouldn't have, only your pony has friends from the stable back home and gave a whicker; that brought us over. But, if I may be so bold, what are you doing here?'

James explained how he had travelled inland to intercept them.

The castle captain shook his head in disapproval and then shrugged. 'Well, it wasn't in my orders to send you home, so you'd best come with us. If we get even half the number of cattle we're looking for we'll need all the cowhands we can muster.'

James bristled at being called a cowhand, but was relieved not to be sent home. The captain relaxed then, and let James ride beside him. 'I have letters of introduction from your father to O'Neill's tenants, and a request that they yield to us the cattle that is due on their rents, but I suspect it will be like getting blood from a stone. Your father was a hero after Kinsale, but I reckon the thought of giving anything to the king, let alone Chichester, will stick in their throats.'

'What if they don't cooperate?' asked James.

The captain reined back so they could talk in private. 'My instructions are to take what we can and explain later. We can't expect a welcome.'

'Yesterday I heard something that might be of interest,' said James. 'I was told by a local that there is a big muster of cattle somewhere north of here. Do you think they got wind of us and are moving their cattle north to be out of our reach? Our work would be half-done if we could surprise them.'

'Well, lad, that *is* interesting. If you're right, they will likely be well guarded. I think I'll send a scout ahead to see what we're up against.'

Just before dusk the captain called the whole party to order. 'This is the plan. The cattle are gathered in a large clearing in the forest ahead. There must be a hundred and fifty there. They seem to have been there for some days, probably mustered so they can be driven north out of our reach. There are herdsmen at intervals about the clearing, but they don't seem to be expecting trouble. You will probably spot them at night by their camp-fires. Their main camp is to the north, which is strange if that's the way they're driving, but there may be some reason for it. I propose to split our party into two. I will lead our better-horsed men in a loop around the herd to attack their camp, cut loose their horses, knock down their tents, beat a few backsides, and make a lot of noise. The rest of you will work on foot and in pairs. You will locate the herdsmen, and then wait for a musket shot that will tell you we are attacking the camp. You will then overpower the guards. Remember, all of you, that these men are not our enemies, they are just tax dodgers. I want no loss of life. Use the flat of your swords if you have to defend yourselves. Any questions?'

'May I ride with you?' asked James.

'No, son, sorry. I could never face your father if you were injured. You will guard the horses we're leaving behind. There's a small clearing just off the road that will be our base.'

James opened his mouth to protest, saw the look on the captain's face, and clamped his jaw. At least he hadn't been sent home.

Night was falling as the raiders moved north, riding in single file on the grass verge, their hooves thudding softly. This way they could melt into the forest if anybody came towards them. When they reached the clearing that was to be their base, they made neat piles of all unnecessary equipment, ready for quick retrieval at need. James, determined to do his humble job well, hammered in stakes and roped off a corral for the spare horses. Then, with strips torn from his spare shirt, he went over to the captain's horses, binding links and buckles to muffle any clinks that might give warning of their coming. As soon as they were ready, the raiders moved away, dark shadows melting silently into the forest. The foot soldiers set off a little later to begin to locate the guards around the herd. James was left alone.

He eased his sword in its scabbard and listened to the night sounds against the distant lowing of cattle. He moved among the horses, talking to them, checking their tethers, fondling their ears. While he was doing this, silent as a cat on soft paws, the moon rose above the trees and flooded the clearing with silver light. He could see a mouse, caught unawares in the open; for one fateful second it sat there, twitching its whiskers. Then, with a silent whoosh, it was gone, and the owl that had taken it rose above the trees.

Time wore on. James explored every inch of the clearing until he knew every bump and hollow on its surface. It had probably once been someone's small-holding. Ridges crossed it where a vegetable garden had once been.

That's it! The musket shot – the signal. James's stomach

tightened into a knot. Distant shouts – another shot – then nothing. Were the cattle lowing more? Or less? Now a sound ... he cocked his head. *Horse's hooves, surely?* A smile of relief grew on his face. *Success!* The hooves were closing fast now. *But those are pony's hooves* – James was alert – *and we don't have any ponies apart from mine*. The patter of hooves on the forest floor slowed. Suspicion pricked his neck, his spine; he put his hand to his sword and stepped out into the clearing.

At that moment a pony came into sight, picking its way delicately through the lush grass. Recognition hit James like an arrow between the eyes.

'Fion O'Neill,' he called, 'dismount! Your challenge still stands. We have unfinished business between us. Are you armed?'

'So, you have turned cattle thief, James de Cashel. Yes, I am armed, but stand back while I tether Bracken here.'

They stood, swords glinting cold in the moonlight and went through a ritual of stroke and counter stroke, both clumsy for lack of practice. Soon, however, they warmed to their work.

James was confident; he had always been the better swordsman. Hadn't he disarmed Fion the last time they had fought? Also, he knew the ground inside the clearing and that would be an advantage, though Fion could surprise. Let the fight start in earnest. He was ready.

'When you're ready – if ever!' mocked Fion.

And James rose to the challenge and fell on Fion like a fury. Their swords flashed in the cold light until they seemed to spin a web around them. *Fion is good, but I am better!* James chanted to himself. All he needed now was one small mistake from Fion and he would have him. He had been forcing Fion back and back; now James pretended that he was tiring, and began to retreat himself, feeling the ground behind him with his feet. There! The first of the old plough furrows. Without showing any sign of what was underfoot, he glided over it, lowering his sword – like a bird feigning a broken wing, drawing Fion on. In a second, Fion would trip and the fight would be over. James wiggled his sword as a child might entice a kitten. *Now!* As if in slow motion, he saw Fion lurch, as his foot caught on the ridge and he begin to pitch forward. Mesmerised by his own success, James watched him topple. But Fion didn't fall. James could only look as Fion converted his fall into a dive. Then throwing his sword aside, he reached out and grabbed the hilt of James's sword. *That's cheating!* thought James as Fion's hands clamped on his like two vices, the force of the boy's dive throwing him back. As he fell, James felt his sword wrenched from his hand. In a second they were both on their feet, but now Fion was holding James's sword.

'Surrender!' Fion demanded.

James could only stare at his empty hands. Fion's discarded sword glinted invitingly from the grass, but Fion saw his eyes move.

'Don't even think of it,' he snapped. 'Surrender, James de Cashel – admit defeat, and declare that our quarrel is over, now and forever.'

'I surrender,' said James; he had no alternative.

'And admit defeat!'

James, looking up the length of his opponent's sword, replied reluctantly, 'I admit defeat.'

'And that our quarrel is done; is over—'

But this was too much. 'No, Fion O'Neill, our quarrel is not over, now nor nev—' But James never finished that sentence because at that moment he saw the cold glint of steel as the blade in Fion's hands flashed down, and everything changed.

❦

Fion, still panting from their fight, had held his sword steady, a sliver of deadly steel pointing directly at James's throat. The boy had surrendered, accepted defeat, all Fion needed now was to know that their quarrel was over. One word and he would tap the flat of his sword on James's shoulder, the victor's touch, and their quarrel would be over, obliterated forever. James's 'No' came like a thrust to his heart. *I'll show him what fear is,* he thought and, with that, Fion swung his sword in a sweeping arc, meaning to bring the blade whistling down to pass a bare inch from James's shoulder. But it wasn't a bare inch. Perhaps James's sword was an inch longer than his own, perhaps it was a trick of the moonlight – certainly James never flinched – but Fion felt his blade meet flesh, saw the black slit in James's shirt, and saw the swift spread of blood through the linen. With an involuntary cry, he leapt forward, throwing the sword aside.

'James, brother, I didn't mean it!' He pulled out his kerchief and frantically clapped it over James's wound. Then he wrapped his arm about him as if by holding him close he could somehow stop the flow. It was minutes before he dared to look at the wound, lifting his kerchief momentarily to judge the depth and extent of it. It was, in fact, hardly more than an inch long but it was deep, and the blood welled up quickly as soon as the pressure was released. He replaced the kerchief and held on to James as before, fighting back huge sobs of regret. Then at last he felt James relax, and realised that he too was crying, not from pain, but from relief – patting Fion on the back, telling him, as he couldn't in words, that their quarrel was over. And so they stood until he heard James say, a little weakly, 'If you don't mind, Fion, I think I'd like to sit down.'

The boys sat side by side until the moon handed night over to day. At some stage, Fion did a proper bandaging job on James's wound. He hardly noticed when James's captain returned, red-faced, to explain how the cattle that they had planned to raid had, in fact, been gathered for them on the orders of Hugh O'Neill.

This was not news to Fion, for only the presence of Hugh O'Neill's nephew, with proper letters of introduction, had persuaded the farmers to give up their cattle, if only in ones or twos. News of Chichester's demands had caught up with the O'Neill party within hours of Chichester's departure, and Uncle Hugh had been furious. 'Three hundred is outrageous, and he knows it. He is just trying to put a wedge between us,' he had stormed, 'and I won't let that happen. And what the devil is this nonsense about Sinéad? Thank God Malachy didn't let Bonmann take her away. That man is evil! He doesn't want *her*, he only wants their land.'

Fion was dispatched immediately.

The boys could hear the shouts as the drovers from both parties drove the cattle from the wide clearing onto the road south. All they wanted for the moment was to sit side by side and talk.

'What did you talk about?' Sinéad asked Fion later. 'Minutes before, you had been deadly enemies.'

'We talked about everything that has happened since Uncle Hugh first brought me to the castle. I would say: Remember...? and before we'd stopped remembering that, James would say: Remember...? On politics, we have agreed to differ. He thinks the days of the Irish chiefs are over and that Chichester is a man of honour. I disagree, obviously.'

When, eventually, it came to moving on, and the boys mounted their ponies, even the ponies seemed to catch their mood and walked close, side by side.

'Will you look at those two lads,' laughed one of O'Neill's cattle men, 'you couldn't see daylight between them.'

CHAPTER 12

Fight or Flight?

attle!' screeched Kathleen, 'hundreds and thousands of them!' Numbers were like corn to Kathleen, the more you scattered the more they grew. Sinéad was out of bed in a second; the raiders must be back! She peered out her bedroom door. Kathleen was standing at the top of the stairs with the jug of hot water that she'd brought up for Mother, slopping it on people in her excitement as they hurried down to see what was going on. Sinéad, still in her night-shift, couldn't follow them, so instead she ran barefoot across the room and up the spiral steps to the battlements where she leaned over. There below, emerging onto the meadow, were not exactly Kathleen's hundreds and thousands, but a goodly stream of cattle.

'How many?' she called up to the watchman on the turret who was counting, a finger raised. He glanced down, saw the young mistress in her shift and quickly looked away. 'Must be close on a hundred and fifty, miss.'

The lowing cattle spread out onto the now browned summer grass, and the drovers delivered their last thumps and shouts. There were horsemen emerging from the forest. Sinéad leaned dangerously over the edge, searching to see if James was there. Had he managed to meet up with the raiders? *There he is!* and she gave a whoop of joy. But who was that on a pony beside him? *It can't be! But look, it is! It's Fion!* She put her fingers into her mouth and gave a whistle that would have brought Saoirse down from the gates of heaven. The boys, dismounted now, looked up as one, squinting against the light, arms over each other's shoulders. They waved. *I can't believe it – they're back – friends!* Half-crying with relief and excitement, Sinéad threw herself down the stairs and was only prevented from haring all the way down by Kathleen catching her about the waist.

'You can't go down like that in your shift, you're stark naked!'

'I'm not naked,' she protested, but her struggle was a mere token as Kathleen began to brush the night tangles out of her hair.

After her first rush of greeting the boys was over, and she had watched as they brushed down and stabled their ponies, word came that James was to attend on his father at once. He went off with a long face, expecting the full force of Father's wrath for having joined the raid without permission.

'We'll be in the falconry,' the others called, as they took themselves off to Fion's private place in the loft. Sinéad watched Fion greet his falcon, whispering to her in a sort of mouth-music all his own, and she noticed how, as he moved about, he kept touching things as if to reassure himself that they were there and that he was back. He climbed ahead of her into the loft and held the ladder as she climbed. As she emerged he touched her lightly on the cheek.

'Just checking,' he grinned. 'You see, when I rode out of here with Uncle Hugh and Con that day I really thought I would never, ever come back.'

'Tell me, Fion, what happened between you and James?'

Fion thought for a moment before saying, 'Let's wait till James comes back,' and so they sat in silence, listening to the sounds of the village about them. Several times he seemed about to speak, but stopped. Eventually, looking at the floor, he said, 'I hear you had a spot of bother ... with a suitor?'

'*Have*, not *had*. He's not gone away!' She began with the 'beastly *bonham*' joke, but that didn't work; this wasn't a joking matter. So in the end she just told him the story, not forgetting James's public stand that she should be allowed to choose for herself whom she married. 'It isn't any good, though. It looks as though my accepting him may be the only way to save our castle and our land.' She didn't want to cry in front of Fion, but it was he who brushed the first tear from her cheek. It was almost a relief when there were sounds below, and they heard James's voice talking to the falcons. Then they remembered he didn't know about Fion's hide-away up here.

'We're up here, James,' she called. 'Try the ladder in the corner.'

'How was it?' they asked in unison, as his head poked up through the trap door, and he looked around in surprise. Fion patted the bench beside him.

'So this is where you used to hide from me,' said James, punching amiably at Fion to make him move over. Sinéad watched them. *This is like old times.* She crossed her fingers.

James took a deep breath. 'Well, I got it hot and strong for going off on my own, and there were awkward questions about how I found out about the raid.' Sinéad winced, but he laughed. 'I told Father I got the information from the merchant, the one who brought me your note, so you can breathe again. That note you wrote me was great – told me everything I needed to know. I think Father's glad, really, that I showed some initiative. He's looking to thank you, Fion, and Uncle Hugh, of course.'

'When do we drive the cattle out?' Fion asked.

'Father wants to hold on to them for a bit. Chichester's allowing Bonmann to recruit a force of his own to watch this side of the county, and Father's damned if he'll hand over our cattle just to feed Bonmann's private army.'

'If we want fair play from them, you know, we should pay our dues,' commented James.

No change in James's politics then, thought Sinéad, and steered the conversation away. 'So, the *bonham* is still around!' she said as casually as she could. 'What does he want an army for?'

'Father says he's just an adventurer like Sir Walter Raleigh, grabbing land for himself in the king's name. We need law and order, not him.'

'Well, at least he isn't after *me*!'

'Don't you believe it,' chuckled James. 'He's just waiting to shake the tree so's you'll drop into his hands like a ripe apple!'

She winced and noticed that Fion didn't join in his chuckle. 'For that, James, you can tell me what happened between you and Fion. You went away swearing death and destruction, and now come back like two turtle doves. And what happened to your shoulder, James? I'm not blind, you know.'

Turn by turn they told her, correcting and reminding each other as they went, clearly excited at re-living what had happened. *I'd need to be a boy to understand this,* she thought.

'You two poor eejits,' she said when they'd finished. 'Come here, James, and let me look at that shoulder of yours.' She examined it in a shaft of light that came through a broken slate in the falconry roof. 'It looks clean and healthy. I'll ask Old Eileen for an ointment you can put on it.'

'That witch?' objected James.

'Call her that, and she'll turn you into a frog!' snapped Sinéad.

The ointment, made from marsh woundwort, soon cleared the angry edges of the wound, and it healed well.

August was stepping aside for September. The trees, looking tired, would soon take on their autumn colours. The cattle had eaten the grass to a dust bowl, and there was change in the air. Sinéad kept her eyes on the boys; their differences had not gone away. There would be flare-ups, like tongues of flame in gorse, but as quickly as they showed, one of them would throw water on the flames and their squabble would die down. They went everywhere together, and though they never turned her away, Sinéad found herself thinking a little bitterly: *They don't really need me, now, do they? My future's all mapped out. First clean me up, then dress me up, and then marry me off to some rich suitor. I could elope, but who would want to elope with me?*

One late summer's day, deep in gloomy thought, she left the boys and wandered out across the meadow, and so was there at the very moment when a line of three horsemen burst from the forest edge, at the very place where Con had emerged over a month ago. As she watched, one of them, a boy, spurred ahead and came pounding directly towards her.

For a wild moment she thought this was, indeed, young Con. He had Con's crouch, even though he had his feet in long, Norman stirrups. When he saw her, he pulled his pony's head up, leaning far back in his saddle, feet thrust forward.

'Welcome, stranger,' she called.

'Mistress, I have an urgent message for Sir Malachy de Cashel.'

'You have come to the right place.'

'Oh good. Excuse me, miss, but are you from the castle?'

'Sinéad de Cashel at your service,' she smiled, bobbing a curtsy. Now that his pony had settled, she realised why she had thought of

Con; he was a replica of the boy, but older, about a year younger than she was. He slipped from his pony and held out his hand, English fashion.

'I'm John O'Neill, son of Hugh O'Neill, the Earl of Tyrone,' he said. 'I have a secret message for your father, but you'll do.' Sinéad wasn't sure if this was a compliment, but the lad was hastening on, clearly remembering instructions that he had learned by heart. 'There are only three people I am allowed to tell: Sir Malachy de Cashel, my cousin Fion, and Sir Malachy's daughter, Sinéad.'

'Well, you've found me,' she said, turning to walk beside him. 'But shouldn't you tell it to Father first?'

'Oh no, I am to tell the first one of you I see, then if something happens to me the message will be safe.'

Sinéad, amused, scanned the field for the bull, the only possible hazard she could think of, but then decided not to tease the boy. For all his self-importance, she could see that his message was like a hot coal in his hands. 'Very wise,' she said. 'You can tell Father later.'

The boy, relieved, took a deep breath: 'I am to tell you that Father's at Mellifont Abbey at this moment. He's a guest of Sir Garret Moore, who's been my foster father for five years now.'

Sinéad nodded. *Hence the courtly behaviour,* she thought, but said, 'I have heard Uncle Hugh talk of Sir Garret as a dear friend.'

'Oh, the best. But even Sir Garrett does not know what I am about to tell you.' He dropped his voice and glanced around suspiciously at the cows; they weren't listening. 'Two days ago Father got word that a ship had arrived in Rathmullan in County

Donegal to take us all to Spain. When he gets there, he will raise a Spanish army to hunt the English out of Ireland.'

Merciful Heaven! No wonder the boy was nervous! This was news beyond anything she could have imagined. It stopped her in her tracks.

'Uncle Hugh leaving!' she gasped, her own fears flooding in. For all the trouble Uncle Hugh had caused them, it was he who had not only kept the English land-grabbers away from them, but the feuding Irish as well.

'Don't worry, we'll be back,' he said gallantly.

'And young Con? Are you all going?'

'Yes, but that's why I'm here. You see, we don't know where Con is. He should be with his foster family, the O'Brolchains, but they're following their cattle somewhere in the hills, and nobody knows where. I told Father I'd go and find Con, but he says that I must stay with him because Mother would never forgive him if he lost both of us.'

'Perhaps we could help find him?' she said without thinking.

'That's just what Father was hoping – not you, of course, but someone your father can trust. It's so, so secret, you see – if Chichester gets a whiff of it we will be headed off before we can get to the boat.'

And be caught and hanged, Sinéad thought grimly. It wasn't much to ask; they'd surely find someone reliable to search for Con.

'I'm sure we can help, but you must tell Father yourself. How is it that you know the short cut through the plashing?' she asked.

'One of us knows the way. It was tricky because the road was blocked by a whole mass of soldiers.'

'What soldiers?' she asked, suddenly alert.

'Someone called Bonmann exercising his troops. I don't know where they're going.'

'I can tell you that. They're coming here!' she said. 'This is the end of the road.' *Bonmann again!* Her legs felt weak. *With Uncle Hugh gone, who'll look after us?* 'Come quickly, John, you must tell Father and then get on your way.'

<hr />

Father took the news of Uncle Hugh's departure almost as if he'd expected it. 'So they sent a boat in the end,' he said to John. 'Your father will do more for our cause in Spain than he can here. We must do our utmost to find Con for you.'

'It was my brother, Henry, who sent the boat–' began John, but Sinéad interrupted, 'Sorry, John, but tell Father about the army you dodged on the way here.'

Father listened with a growing frown. 'Bonmann, by God!' and at that moment, from somewhere high above, came a sound that sent a thrill down Sinéad's spine: the Great Horn of the de Cashels blowing the alarm.

Father sat up. 'Quickly, boy, tell me roughly where Con's to be found, and then you must go.'

CHAPTER 13

The Great Horn
of the de Cashels

ames sat up from his work when the braying sound of the Great Horn rang out from the battlements above. The breastplate he'd been polishing for Father slipped and crashed to the floor. In a single bound, he leapt over the fallen breastplate and made for the tower steps.

'What? ... Where? ... Who?' he gasped as he reached the look-out, but then had to cover his ears as a second blast rang out. The man on watch, too puffed to speak, pointed to the forest road, where James saw a solid phalanx of horsemen appear. The sunlight glinted on their helmets. *No plumed hats*, thought James, *is this war?* He soon had his answer, for in no time at all the horsemen had spread out to cast a moving net across the meadows. *They're after someone!* he thought, and looked down onto the village below. Everywhere people were responding to the alarm, running towards the safety of the castle from the fields, or out to man the palisade. Father must be told. As he hurtled down the stairs, James felt betrayed. *We're loyal now. Why are they hounding us? If it's the cows they want, why send a whole army?* He forced his way through the bustle at the door and burst into the great hall, where, to his surprise, he found Father talking to Sinéad and a young red-headed lad, who looked vaguely familiar; but he must interrupt.

'Father, excuse me, I've come from the battlements. There are twenty horse or more spreading out from the forest road.'

Father frowned. Signalling for James to wait, he turned to the boy and said: 'Go now, while you can. I have your message and will send a man as soon as the present trouble is over. God's speed!'

The boy ran past James for the door. *That's who he reminds me of,* thought James, *Con O'Neill!*

'Another O'Neill?' he asked, as the boy disappeared. Sinéad opened her mouth to reply, but Father got in first: 'Just a messenger. Thank you, James, for coming so quickly. I have feared this; we must put our defence plan into action. I will move into the guard room now and take command. You, James, will clear the great hall here as a refuge for the women and children. All able-bodied men will take their stations at the palisade with the instructions to fall back on the castle if there is any attack. I want no heroics; we have a castle, let the walls be our defence, understand?'

'But, Father, these are the king's men, why should we have to defend ourselves?'

'Because the king's men don't always fight for the king; they fight for themselves.'

James had no more time for speculation but as he ran to complete Father's orders he couldn't help wondering about that boy. If he was a mere messenger, why would Father wish him 'God's speed' as if he were a nobleman? It was strange.

Sinéad, however, ran after the boy towards the stables, and would have helped him saddle his pony if one of his companions hadn't appeared to help him. *Where have I seen that man before?* she wondered as he calmed and reassured the boy, holding his foot as he swung into the saddle. As the boy rode out he looked down at Sinéad and said, 'I hope you'll be all right.'

'We'll be fine,' she replied. 'Haven't we got four stone walls to hide behind? God's speed,' she added, liking the phrase Father had used. As he cantered off she noticed that the boy had only one companion now. The other was beside her still, watching the boy fondly as the two disappeared into the forest. She turned to look at him. *Of course!* It was the poet who had played that night when Chichester had dined with them. He was looking at her quizzically, one bushy eyebrow raised.

'Am I forgiven?' he said humbly.

'For what, sir?'

'For playing a Sassenach tune that caught you a fish you could have done without.'

Sinéad grimaced. 'Yes, but I don't want to be the jilted lover in one of your songs. Father says: "Never cross a poet." May I ask your name?'

'Young Con called me Haystacks. The name tickles me.'

'I'd say it does. You'd better come into the safety of the castle. My suitor is about to attack.'

'I will come, but first I would like a word with one, Fion O'Neill. Do you know him?'

⁂

Fion recognised their visitor from Sinéad's description. 'I've heard he's a poet, and a harper too,' he said, 'but I've never worked out if he's Uncle Hugh's poet, or if he's just a poet who's adopted Uncle Hugh. If he's here, we can be sure it's about Uncle Hugh's business, whether Uncle Hugh knows it or no.'

Sinéad introduced him to Fion as Mr Haystacks, and then excused herself, sensing that their talk would be private.

⁂

As she walked back to the castle from the stables, Sinéad felt as if the weight of the world had landed on her shoulders. This was like a stage play, to be repeated whenever the English fancied it: fleeing friends, approaching horsemen, marching men. *If only there was something I could do that would send them all away* ... At that moment she knew, and knew clearly! She stopped in her tracks. *Oh dear God give me courage!*

❦

When Fion and the stranger were alone he said: 'Your uncle thinks well of you, Fion, so I won't beat about the bush. I could have spirited you away with John just now, leaving your young fosterlings to fend for themselves, but my guess is that you would prefer to stay?'

'Yes, sir!'

'In that case, let's prepare for all eventualities. We'll steal some horses together for a start.'

❦

James, watching the advance of the horsemen from the castle tower, never noticed four ponies and a horse being quietly led away into the woods behind him. He did, however, wonder who the boy was who had been talking to Father, and whether he had got away. Meanwhile the approaching horsemen were wasting no time, and soon the castle was effectively surrounded by a vigilant ring of horsemen circling the palisade, just beyond bow-shot. For the time being they made no attempt to close in. All they did was to arrest and question a couple of herdsmen caught hurrying home in answer to the Great Horn.

'There, sir, there!' growled the watchman beside James, pointing to the forest road. 'Foot soldiers, a hundred by the look.' James squinted, trying to make his own estimate, but it was impossible to see how many there were, or what they had with them because of the dust they raised. As he hurried down to see Father, the Great Horn rang out again.

It took the foot soldiers twenty minutes to reach the castle, a formidable force of men that, like the horsemen, drew up a safe bow-shot from the palisade where they seemed busy, as if they were making preparations for a long stay. They even pitched a tent at their centre. A messenger came forward from their ranks.

'Go to the palisade gate, James, and report what he has to say,' ordered Father.

James went and returned quickly.

'Well, boy, who is it? If it had been Sir Arthur himself I'd have come to the door–'

'No sir, as we know, but Sir Geoffrey Bonmann. You'll remember he–'

'Indeed! Well, what's that upstart doing coming here to menace me? Who's he acting for and what does he want? Tell him he has no right to Chichester's cattle!'

'He claims we're harbouring Hugh O'Neill, sir.'

'Well, we're not!'

'He says the king is calling O'Neill to London over his land dispute with O'Cahan.'

'Land dispute, be damned! The king wants to cut off his head!

First Chichester, and now this Bonmann chap – do they think I run a hotel for the O'Neill clan here?' James was about to comment on that, but bit it off. His father went on. 'Tell him that O'Neill's in the garderobe at the moment and can't be disturbed ...' but then he sighed, 'No ... no ... I'd better see him. Clear the guard room. I'll talk to him there in private. You wait outside.'

⸻

James stood on guard with his back to the door, straining to hear what was being said inside. It was frustrating; he could hear Father quite clearly, but Bonmann's lisping tones came as a whisper. He barely heard Bonmann's accusation about O'Neill and grinned at Father's angry denials, but now they were talking cattle.

Father's voice rose. 'Those cattle are due to Sir Arthur Chichester, not to you, sir!' James strained to hear how Bonmann replied, but all he heard was Father's angry response. 'Don't give me that legal clap-trap! Damn you to hell,' Father roared, 'you thieving, land-grabbing upstart. You will NOT take my castle, NOR my land, by any legal dodge or thievery. Get out of here and get off my land – even better, get out of Ireland or I will get Hugh O'Neill to beat the lard out of you.' Then Father switched to Irish, using words that James had only heard from the cattlemen at cockfights.

When the door opened behind him, James nearly fell back into Bonmann's arms, and found himself pushed disdainfully aside, as the man swept towards to the castle door.

Suddenly, the man stopped dead in his tracks. James looked past him, and gaped.

There stood Sinéad, dressed in Uncle Hugh's gorgeous dress, standing like Queen Maeve, defying the man to pass. She held her ground, chin cocked, blocking his exit. James stepped forward, determined to protect her, but Sinéad needed no protection.

'Sir,' she said, loud enough for all to hear. 'I am ready to come with you, here and now, and when old enough, to become your wife, on condition that you take your army now and leave our castle and our lands, and never return.'

The man stood as if struck, but it only lasted a second. Immediately the suave charm returned. Bonmann stepped forward and bent down to Sinéad's level – to kiss her? – to sweep her up and carry her away? No, it was to whisper in her ear.

But James heard, and it was like a knife thrust between his ribs.

'First your castle, then your lands, and then you, my sweetheart – then *you* will be the jewel in my crown!'

Bonmann stood up, but not quickly enough to avoid Sinéad's stinging slap. Then he was off and down the steps to return to his army.

James's first instinct was to lunge after the man and challenge him to fight; his second was to throw his arms around his sister, but she was like a firecracker and in no mood for hugs.

'James!' called his father from inside the guard room. 'Come here, we have work to do.'

Sinéad's fury carried her up the stairs without touching the walls. Once up, however, her fury deserted her. She fled to her room, closed the door and collapsed in a crumpled heap as her anger turned to shame. *I offered myself to that creep!* Her only satisfaction was her stinging palm.

She must have slept then because the next thing she heard was Fion's voice coming urgently through the door.

'Sinéad, you are to come. Your father's called a family meeting.'

She looked down at her now hateful finery. 'I must change. I'm in this stupid costume.'

'No. Come as you are. Bonmann may attack at any minute. Find your mother and bring her to the guard room.' Sinéad found Mother in the great hall marking out sleeping places for the families from the village.

'Oh, my child, you're not dressed up for Sir Geoffrey, are you?' Mother asked. Sinéad didn't trust her voice to reply, she just led Mother by the hand into the guard room.

Fion closed the door; he was one of the family here. They sat on the benches that lined the walls.

Father, looking drawn but grim, began: 'You all realise that we are now under siege. A short time ago I had a visit from – it galls me to give him the title – *Sir* Geoffrey Bonmann. He has presented me with a list of false accusations and demands, none of which would stand up in a court of law. When I asked if he was here on

Chichester's business he was evasive, and I see no just reason for him being here.'

'Father, I can!' said Sinéad bitterly. 'There is no reason, no plot – just greed. He told me himself, he wants our castle, then our lands, and I am to be thrown into the bargain.'

'Oh, come now, child, how could you possibly know this? That's nonsense!'

'With respect, sir, it's true!' said James, rising like a fighting cock. 'When Sir Bonmann left you, Sinéad blocked his way out there by the castle door, and said loud enough for me to hear that she would agree to be his bride if he would take his army away and never, ever come back. And this was his reply: "First your castle, then your lands, then *you* will be the jewel in my crown."'

Father, stunned, turned to Sinéad. 'You did this, Sinéad? Dressed up and did it for us? I thought you didn't like him?'

Her answer was a whisper. 'I loathed him before, and I loathe him now!'

Father looked at her as if seeing his daughter for the first time. 'Well then, I think we must keep this jewel for our own crown. We have enough food to hold off a siege for a good few weeks. I'll get word out to Chichester. I'm sure he'll put a stop to this man's gallop–'

There was a knock on the door. Father nodded to James to answer it. There was a murmur of conversation. James stepped out for a moment. When he returned, his face looked drained.

'Father, I'm afraid the situation has changed. Bonmann has

brought up a cannon and it is now trained on the castle door.'

Father sat back with a grunt. 'Without the door we don't have enough men to hold the castle.'

Mother spoke. 'Sir Malachy, can't we just invite him in, show him that O'Neill is not hiding here, and tell him to take Chichester's cattle and go away?'

'The trouble is, my dear, that he won't go. He's an adventurer, a man without honour. He wants our castle and our lands for himself, and will stop at nothing to grab them. This is how the English are conquering Ireland, sowing our castles with English aristocracy, and our land with their peasants. After poor Desmond lost his war in Munster they planted his land with English settlers like seed-corn. We chased them out, and now they're back again. Our only protection now is the law. If I can persuade him to put a cannon ball through the door in an unprovoked attack, we will at least have a case against him. Unfortunately, there's a flaw to this proposal – three flaws, to be precise.'

'What, Sir Malachy? I don't understand,' said Mother.

'The jewels in *our* crown, my dear. First there is Fion, nephew of Hugh O'Neill; if he's caught we'll be accused of harbouring the enemy and he'll be handed over to Chichester as a very useful hostage. Then there is James, our son and heir, to be clapped in irons in Dublin Castle on some trumped-up charge to force me to drop my case against Bonmann. Then, last but not least, there is Sinéad. There are things called forced marriages, and I will not have that on my conscience. No, he has us over a barrel now. If I could spirit the three of you out of here I'd be free to negotiate.'

It was Fion who spoke next. 'Sir, I will give myself up to him. I will say that you held me captive—'

But Sir Malachy stopped him. 'No, boy, you won't – but by God, we have nobler children here than there are men outside. James, you have something to say?'

'Yes, sir. You may remember telling me years ago that there had once been a tunnel between the castle and the fairy fort?'

'Yes, and I told you never to go there. Dangerous place, that's why I scared you off. It's not accessible, you know.'

'I remember your tales, sir: ghosts, ghouls, and even the fairy folk themselves. I'm afraid I disobeyed you, sir. I explored the tunnels made by the ancients. One of them led me back towards the castle. It had collapsed, but I cleared it. It comes up into the undercroft.'

'I should thrash you for disobedience, boy,' said Father, 'only that when I was a lad I was told never to go there – so, of course, I too disobeyed. The difference is that you have succeeded where I failed! Is the exit beyond the cordon of men?'

'The far side is beyond the cordon, I believe. Anyway, the soldiers are Irish. They know a fairy fort when they see one and will avoid it.'

'Well, you and Fion must get ready to leave at once. We may not have much time. Fion has an urgent job to do for his uncle and I suggest you help him with that. I will give you instructions on where to go after that. But the woods are no place for a wandering girl, Sinéad, so I'm afraid we'll have to put you in the priest's hole and hide you here.'

‘Cut it off, Kathleen!' shouted Sinéad.

‘I can't, missy – your beautiful hair!'

‘I said CUT IT OFF. Look, I'll do it myself,' and Sinéad seized the shears from Kathleen's hands and hacked off a ragged lock.

‘Oh stop! You'll kill yourself.'

‘Well, you do it so. Use the pudding bowl like you use on the boys. I want a boy's cut, not some fancy girly job.' Giggling with nervous laughter, Kathleen set to while Sinéad closed her eyes against the black silken carpet that was gathering about her feet. While Kathleen snipped, she issued more orders.

‘I want clothes, Kathleen, boy's clothes, the older the better. Oh God, and I'll need boots too.'

‘Will you be taking your new dress?'

‘Kathleen, you eejit, don't you understand? I'm running *away* from the beastly *bonham*. It's like eloping, but in reverse. The boys are coming too.' And in case Kathleen might be worried for her own safety, she told her that there would be no fight. It was just that Father wanted her and the boys out of the way. Fortunately, Kathleen was too taken up with her cutting to ask how they would leave. Eventually the maid stood back to admire her work, put her hand over her mouth and let out a snort of laughter.

‘Stop laughing, Kathleen! This is important. Now I need

clothes – old ones, but get me clean ones, please!'

The shearing had taken place in the privacy of the guest room, one of the few rooms with a fireplace. While Kathleen went off to raid the boys' chests for clothes, Sinéad went to the chimney, and, kneeling in the grate, felt the inside of the chimney above her for a smear of soot. She was more successful than she'd hoped. There was a whoosh and she staggered back, coated in black from head to foot. Choking, she rubbed diligently at it, blackening her face and hands. Kathleen came in with an armful of plundered clothes.

'Holy smoke, will you look at the creature – my first black girl!' she exclaimed, as she stripped off Sinéad's shift and dropped it on the floor. 'Try these ...' She stood back, still trying not to laugh while Sinéad tried on various well-worn, but, on the whole, clean garments. Later she would thank Kathleen in her heart for having forced her into clothes that seemed far too hot for the time of year. 'If you're going to be out at night, you'll need wool next to the skin,' she'd declared.

Sinéad hadn't realised how rough and coarse boy's clothes would feel. It took careful selection, but in the end she had drawers, a woollen vest that tickled, patched trousers, a greyish linen shirt, and a short tunic such as country boys wore. She needed a cloak. Kathleen went off and was back in a minute. 'Look, miss, I've found this old one in the garderobe.' She held up a mottled cloak, and despite the disgust on Sinéad's face, she rolled it up firmly. 'You'll take it, young miss, and be grateful for it!' She helped Sinéad make a pack of her spare clothes. When, however, she looked at the forlorn pile of

Sinéad's beautiful hair and Uncle Hugh's dress thrown over the table, she lost her nerve and wailed: 'What have I done – where's my little girl?' and gave Sinéad a huge and tearful hug. 'The Mistress will eat me, and you don't even feel right!'

Sinéad, beginning to choke up, pushed her away. 'Give Bonmann a lock of my hair – with my love.'

'Oh no, miss,' said Kathleen, practical at once, 'sure that might tell him to go looking for a boy.'

Somehow I don't think he will, thought Sinéad.

***

Father had left the guard room to talk to the guard, and Fion now faced James across the small table that had been brought in for Father to work at.

'Well, James,' Fion asked, 'will you come with me, then?'

James's mind was in turmoil. He had staked everything on his dream of English rule. 'Fion,' he said, 'I'll show you the way out, but I'll leave you then. I'm convinced that Chichester knows nothing about Bonmann's attack. I'll ride south and appeal to him to call Bonmann off. I refuse to believe that Chichester is behind this.

***

Kathleen brought Sinéad the news that the boys were ready. Without telling anyone, she had made an extra pack of provisions which she now gave to Sinéad, who thanked her with a hug before making her way downstairs.

Sinéad hesitated outside the guard room door then pushed it open and slipped in.

Father looked up. 'Hey you, boy, not in here. Into the great hall with you.'

Sinéad held her ground, then said loudly and, she hoped, confidently, 'Father! I have decided I am going with the boys.' She walked forward into the room. There was a gasp of surprise.

Mother let out a shriek: 'Sinéad! Your hair! Your beautiful–'

'Quiet, woman!' interrupted Father. 'Come here, boy ...' and he scrutinised her. 'Well, I'm blowed, it *is* you, Sinéad.' There was a long pause and everyone looked at Father. 'I really don't know,' he said finally, 'but it could be the answer.'

'Don't let her go, Sir Malachy!' pleaded Mother.

But Father turned to the boys. 'Well, will you take her?'

'As far as I'm concerned, yes, but she mustn't slow us down,' said Fion.

Father looked at her – a look that seemed to search deep inside her. His eyes warmed. 'I think she'll keep up, and if she doesn't, she'll make up for it with sound sense.' He turned to the boys. 'Come, boys, my blessing.' He placed his hands on their heads in turn. Then he looked at Sinéad and laughed. 'You, too – I'll name you Brian, Sinéad. It is an honourable name, don't disgrace it. Now you must learn to kneel like a boy – anyway, you're too sooty for a kiss.'

But Mother had no such scruples.

CHAPTER 14

Tunnels and Old Bones

inéad was terrified, last in the line, crawling on hands and knees down the tunnel that James had found, leading from the castle undercroft to the fairy fort. It was awkward crawling with all her possessions slung around her neck. If only the boys would wait for her! Hot wax from her candle suddenly tipped onto her hand, and instinctively she let it go. The candle flared for a second, then died as the last glimmer of Fion's candle ahead disappeared around a corner. Blackness such as she had never known enveloped her. Her short shout of terror was absorbed by the darkness, and she was alone with Father's stories of ghosts and ghouls and fairies.

Or was she alone? There, behind her – a grunt – a shuffle. *Dear God, what is it?* Terror reached out and ran its claws down her back. She was last in the line, but yet, without a doubt, something large was pushing through the narrow tunnel behind her. She tried to scuttle forward on hands and knees, but immediately tripped over her pack. She turned. She could see it now in a sudden glow in the tunnel – a great shaggy creature, like a bear. She let out a stifled shriek. The bear stopped. *Stupid!* she thought. *Bears don't carry candles, but what could it be?*

'Is that you, Sinéad, or should I say Brian?'

'Yes!' she squeaked.

'I'm Haystacks. Where's your candle?'

'Dropped it!'

'And the boys?'

'Gone on.'

'I'm joining you, all right?'

'Oh yes, please do!' In her relief she wanted to hug the furry creature, but he was being strictly practical. He found her candle on the floor, lit it from his, and explained briefly how Father had asked him to see them to safety. She could see now he was wearing the shaggy Wexford mantle that Con had mistaken for a haystack.

'This is the easiest way of carrying it,' he explained.

❧

'Where did you get to, Sinéad?' demanded the boys when Sinéad caught up with them. Then, seeing the lumbering form behind her, 'Stop there! Who ... what are you? Go back!'

'Put your daggers away, boys, I'm just something ancient that Sinéad disturbed in the tunnels.'

James recognised him. 'I know you. You're the poet who played the harp at our feast for the English!'

'The very man,' said Haystacks, shuffling forward.

Sinéad could see now that they were in a chamber where several tunnels met. It was a relief to be able to sit upright.

'I hear you've found a way through this maze?' Haystacks continued.

'Yes, sir,' said James respectfully. 'At the moment we are under the very centre of the ancient fort. It's a short climb from here up to the roots of the great hawthorn in the middle.'

'Is there no exit closer to the woods?'

'Well … yes … sort of.' James sounded doubtful.

'Well?'

'Beside the fort there's a tomb that even the ancients never entered. I broke in once by mistake and found a tunnel lined with stone slabs and a chamber with bones – human bones in a cupped stone. The place was full of ghosts.' He shivered. 'I even heard unearthly voices and panicked. Luckily the badgers had broken in on the far side, so I was able to escape. But I don't want to go back.'

'I echo your respect, James, but the only bones you need to fear are living ones, and it wouldn't surprise me if the voices you heard weren't real voices coming through the badgers' entrance. How far is it to the forest from the badgers' set?'

'A hundred paces, at a guess, sir.'

'You'll be seen, for sure, as the moon will be bright. But it's the best route. We need to create a diversion. I will climb up into the fort while you crawl through to your tomb. When you hear an unearthly voice, that will be me, and it will be your chance to run. Fion will lead you to where we tied your ponies and a place where you can rest. Before you go, however, here's a piece of advice: from now on when you travel, remember your first duty is always to the person *behind* you on the path, not in front. That way, no one will get left behind. God knows what Sinéad will stir up next if she's left on her own!'

<hr />

Sinéad clamped her arms between her knees to stop her candle from shaking. Forcing her eyes open, she gazed cautiously around the chamber. This was the scariest place she had ever been. It was quite small and the sides were huge vertical slabs of stone. Above her was a single immense slab that covered the roof. And there, in the centre of the tomb, was the cup-shaped stone with its pathetic pile of blackened bones. They were quite small, like sticks from around a bonfire. *A girl, perhaps – like me!* An unexpected draught made her candle flicker. 'I'm sorry!' she whispered to the unquiet spirit, shielding her flame with a cupped hand, but the others had noticed the draught too.

'That'll be Haystacks opening the exit in the fort,' James whispered. Sure enough, somewhere out there in the darkness a voice began to chant a lament, a high, weird sound, music with embedded words.

'Come on!' said James, 'that's Haystacks. We must go!'

They moved towards the exit. But suddenly there was a patter of feet and a burst of Irish from outside: 'God almighty, I'm getting out of here, the place is bewitched. I've had enough of soldiering, I'm for home.' Two soldiers crashed into the bushes outside the chamber. The children quickly blew out their candles and pulled back into the darkness.

'But there are officers following us,' said the second soldier.

'Quiet!' said the first.

The children could clearly hear the thud of boots over the heavy breathing of the two deserters.

'Where did those layabouts go?' said a voice in English. But at that moment Haystacks's lament rose again. 'There's that call! Prime your pistol! Come on!' and the feet thudded off into the distance.

There were surreptitious sounds from where the two deserters were hiding just a few feet away from the children. There was a whisper in Irish. 'I reckon if we lie low here, Sean, we'll get away.'

The three children stared at their only exit in dismay. Something must be done. Then, in a flash, they all had the same thought. Fion began it with a note as low as he could muster; James joined in, and together their cry rose into a wavering wail. When Sinéad joined in, swooping down from a high note, there wasn't a man or woman in Ireland who wouldn't have run for their lives like those two soldiers!

'Now!' whispered Fion.

One after another they squeezed out to find themselves kneeling in the soft bedding that the badgers had cleaned out of their set. A brief look left and right, and off they sprinted across the moonlit meadow. A musket shot rang out, but it wasn't aimed at them. Half-way across both Fion and James remembered Haystacks's instructions and looked back, but Sinéad was right there with them. They reached the forest, melted into the trees and were safe.

CHAPTER 15

Changed Utterly

hey crouched, still trembling from their escape, within the trees and bushes at the forest edge.

'Do you think they got Haystacks?' worried Sinéad.

'There were several shots,' said James.

Fion, who had slipped away to try to find the path to where the ponies had been hidden, reappeared. 'I've found them. Come on. We should get away from here.'

But James was having second thoughts. 'I think I should go back. If there's to be an attack, I should be at Father's side.'

'Nonsense!' said Sinéad. 'You heard Father say that if they took you as hostage, they would use you against him. He doesn't need that – and he doesn't need fighting men now,' she added generously.

She felt Fion's hand on her arm. 'Come on. Sinéad, you walk in the middle.'

'How did you know we'd need the ponies?' she asked his receding back.

'Haystacks guessed your father would want us out of the way.'

'Can we trust him?' James asked from behind.

'Uncle Hugh trusts him and that's good enough for me.' And Fion set off at a brisk pace.

They walked, like badgers, in a line, each lost in their own thoughts. Last year's leaves whispered about their ankles. Would they have a home to go back to when they had found Con? Would Chichester listen to James if he found him? After a short walk, the eager whicker of their ponies welcomed them. Sinéad hugged her pony's warm neck and breathed in the rich, horsey smell.

'Where did you and Haystacks arrange to meet?' James asked Fion.

'The Fiddler's Hill. We'll rest there to see what happens. Maybe you two will be able to return home, but Haystacks and I must leave at dawn to find Con.'

The Fiddler's Hill rose out of a clearing in the forest, a rocky knoll that looked down on the castle below. It had got its name from a long-dead fiddler – his wife, having no ear for music, had hunted him from the house to practise up here. People swore you could still hear his haunting tunes on clear evenings.

When they reached their meeting point they set about making a shelter out of green branches. It was big enough for three, but James was far too agitated to sleep, so he told Fion and Sinéad to get some rest, promising to wake them if anything happened.

James selected a small exposure of rock and settled to wait for the attack on the castle, but was unable to sit still. Like a caged animal, he began walking up and down, and soon had worn a path for himself through the ferns. *What am I expecting? Will I hear it from up here?* He strained his eyes, trying to make out the castle. The campfires of the attacking troops had sunk to pinpricks. *What was that?* A stab of fire had shot out from the blackness below. Then it came, a roar loud enough to make his insides tighten. He waited and waited. *That can't be all?* Another stab of flame, another gut-wrenching bang. *Missed once, missed twice.* He almost cheered, but then, at the third shot, he heard shouts below. Now lights were springing up in an arc across the plane as the attacking soldiers plunged their torches into their camp-fires so that their comrades could see to re-load their muskets. He heard the deadly rattle of musket fire, and there were counter flashes from the palisade as the castle defenders returned fire.

James imagined himself down there leading a counter charge when – *Oh dear God, no!* He covered his ears, trying to block out a sound that hadn't been heard in four hundred years: the call of Great Horn of the de Cashels sounding the retreat. He sank to his knees in the ferns and wept. Then out of sheer exhaustion, he slept.

He woke an hour later, and got stiffly to his feet. His woollen cloak was drenched with dew. He shook it and glared angrily down at the grey bulk of the castle below. Then he looked again. A tiny spark of light showed. *What's that? A flame on the castle tower?*

A signal? A beacon, perhaps? Careful, he thought, *you'll set the place on fire!* And he was right. That was exactly what was happening. *I don't believe what I'm seeing ...*

'Fion! Sinéad!' he yelled. 'The castle's on fire. They've set the castle on fire! Come quickly!'

The fierce orange glow now seemed to be the only light in the universe.

∽≈∾

Dazed with sleep, unaware even that the attack had happened, Sinéad and Fion struggled from their shelter. They could see James, his front eerily lit red from a glow below, and rushed over. The castle – *their* castle – was ablaze. They watched in horror as the glow changed from yellow to red and flames sprang up to dance mockingly above their old home.

'Oh my God!' whispered Sinéad. 'Father ... Mother. Could they be trapped in the top floor?'

'It must be an accident,' James reassured her. 'The only fire-places are in the top floor. They'd be the first to notice – I'm sure they've had time to get out.' The climax passed amazingly quickly – the flames burst upwards as the floors inside collapsed, then drew back, leaving a crown of orange, while the thick walls hid the furnace within. They could see the windows as scarlet slits in the black walls.

The children clung together like sailors on a sinking ship.

When dawn was still only a promise in the sky, Sinéad thought she would start down the track to see if there was any sign of Haystacks. He was to have followed them to the Fiddler's Hill, but hadn't arrived. She came on him not far below the clearing, leading his horse. Haystacks didn't say anything to begin with, just put his arm across her shoulder. As they got to the brightness of the glade she looked up with a smile, but the smile froze on her lips. His face, capable of so many moods, was now etched with grief, and she knew it was on her behalf. A dreadful chill ran through her. He reached across and turned her till she was facing him.

'Father ... Mother ...?' she whispered.

'Sinéad, my dear, it's bad news. Alas, they didn't get out of the castle in time. They had no chance.' He closed his eyes for a moment as if seeing it all again. 'I was trapped down there and got mixed in with the attackers. I saw it all. I last saw your father fighting his way up the stairs. I like to think that he and your mother died in each other's arms.' He closed his cloak around Sinéad as she collapsed against him, shaking with grief.

Later, they all sat on the rock where James had held his night vigil and gazed down at the dimming glow from the castle, now a funeral pyre. Sinéad's shakes were sporadic now. She searched for Fion's hand from under Haystacks's cloak and clamped on to it tightly. As if her touch had opened a dam in him, tears streamed down his face too, and she knew that he shared her sadness.

After a while James left them and began to pack his clothes and harness his pony as if preparing for a journey. 'Haystacks, I won't be coming with you,' he announced. 'You see, I must be avenged for what happened down there before I can grieve properly. You two are lucky, you can cry. My only hope of justice is to appeal to Milord Chichester.'

Haystacks stood up. 'Come, James, spare me a minute.' He turned to the others too. 'Listen, all of you. There are things I learned last night that shocked even an old cynic like me. It's time you all knew the truth about what happened down there. Sit down and I will tell you what I know.

'You all know that Chichester has a loathing of your Uncle Hugh that goes back to when his brother was killed years ago in a skirmish with one of Hugh's followers? Over the years, this hatred has extended to all your Uncle's friends, including Sir Malachy de Cashel. Only the king's pardon stopped him from arresting your father, James, and taking all your land. Instead, he recruited Fenton to act as a spy in your household with instructions to recruit you, James, to the English cause. It was Fenton who sent Chichester word of Uncle Hugh's visit that time when Con rode in to warn us.'

James put his head on his knees, remembering the pig-swill man's message, "They're coming, Master!" and then how Fenton had suddenly changed his tune, wanting Uncle Hugh to stay so that Chichester would catch him surely. *How was I so blind?*

'Who burned the castle then? It obviously wasn't Bonmann,' James asked. 'Remember, Sinéad, how he said: "First your castle, then your land...?"'

'No, it wasn't Bonmann,' said Haystacks. 'It was Chichester.'

There was a stunned silence. 'When Chichester saw that Bonmann wanted your castle, he let him raise his private troop, and even gave him a cannon to help do the job. Once he had ousted your father, however, Bonmann's usefulness was over. The last thing Sir Arthur wanted was to have the castle in the hands of an idiot like Bonmann, who could lose it to us Irish any day. Better to torch it so no one could use it.'

'But... but... Chichester wasn't there. Who...?'

'Someone who knew the castle backwards, someone you all know.'

James's mouth dropped open. 'Fenton?'

'Who else? He came as a member of Bonmann's troop, but was under Chichester's orders. I suspect that these orders were to burn the castle – and Bonmann too, if he had the chance. Bonmann only just got out.'

Sinéad began to cry. 'They're all so horrid. I want to go down,' she whimpered. 'I want to see Mother and Father properly buried. I want to know that all the people who worked for us are all right. What about Kathleen?'

'You're right, of course, Sinéad. But just now you three are in the most terrible danger. Don't you see, Chichester wants Fion as a hostage to keep Uncle Hugh in order. Bonmann wants you and James out of the way so he can take your lands for himself. But possibly most dangerous of all is Fenton. He is a murderer, and murderers will murder again to escape discovery. We all know too much for his comfort. At any minute now they will discover that you three did not die in the fire. Any one of them would be a bad enemy, but all three! We must go – and go now. We have one clear instruction and that is to find Con.'

While the others packed for their journey, James, who had already packed for his ride to Chichester, sat staring at the blackened hulk of his former home below.

When they were all ready to go, Haystacks called, 'James, if you're coming with us, we should be on our way.'

James got up and walked stiffly towards them. He stopped a pace or two short of Fion.

'Fion,' he said formally, 'I would like to come with you and to help you to find young Con. I suspect your quest involves more than that, but it will take time before you can trust me. I swear I will not betray you as others have betrayed me.'

There was a murmur of relief.

'But I want to ask one thing,' he continued. 'From now on, I'd like to be known as ... as Séamus.'

For a moment they stood in stunned silence. Sinéad wanted to throw her arms about her brother; she knew that this was a huge turning point for him, but how about Fion and Haystacks – would they understand? Could they trust him?

She turned to Haystacks. 'May we tell him?'

'Fion?' Haystacks asked in turn.

Fion thought for a moment then said: 'We fought a duel for this moment. I would trust Séamus – or even James – with my life. It's going to be really hard to remember your new name, Séamus,' he added, 'but I'm very glad you've chosen it.'

They sat in a circle, heads together and told him of Uncle Hugh's plans.

Now it was time to go. When Sinéad turned to look down on the castle for one last time, something drew her eyes up instead of down. Up and up she looked, searching the vast dome of the sky above, and there she saw a tiny speck. Without thinking, her fingers rose to her mouth; she took a long breath and her shrill whistle climbed to where Saoirse circled above. She saw her beloved falcon stall high above her and then begin his breathtaking descent, and her heart gave a great lurch. She didn't see the horrified faces of her companions, wondering who else might have heard her call, because here was Saoirse levelling his flight and flying straight to her out-held wrist, where he settled proudly.

'Holy smoke, Sinéad, you can't bring a hawk with you!' said Séamus.

Sinéad just shook her head. 'Here Jame– Séamus, I mean, help me! Your dagger – cut his jesses. He's to be free now.' *Like me*, a secret voice whispered inside. 'Quick, I've no gauntlet and his claws are killing me.'

Séamus carefully cut the thin leather thongs that hung from Saoirse's legs; these might indeed have got caught in the trees and bushes where he must now hunt for himself.

Sinéad lifted her arm high. 'God's speed!' she called as Saoirse spread his wings and rose above them, hovering there for a second before wheeling out over his old home.

<hr/>

Down in the castle village, where the fire had not reached, Henry Fenton looked up, startled. *I've heard that whistle before – but it can't be! They're all dead, all three – aren't they?* Then a chill ran down his back. *Perhaps they're not!*

CHAPTER 16

Flight and Freedom

aystacks took charge. 'It is more urgent than ever now for us to move from here.'

Sinéad winced: had her whistle put them all in danger? This was a different Haystacks; she could be listening to Father commanding his men.

'Fion,' he said urgently, 'we are agreed that Con is almost certainly in the Sperrin mountains?' Fion nodded. 'That would normally be three days' ride from here, but, frankly, you don't have that much time. This is now Tuesday, and you must find Con by Thursday at the latest.'

'Why do you say "you" and not "us" – aren't you coming?' Sinéad asked anxiously.

'I'll be with you and not with you,' said Haystacks. 'Three sparrows can fly through a hedge where an old buzzard like me might get stuck. In the old days the forest paths would have been the best, relying on help from the Irish chiefs, and hidden from the English lion. Sadly, many of the chiefs have turned against O'Neill and might well hand you over to the enemy.'

'So it's Irish wolves or English lions!' declared Sinéad.

'It is indeed. The good roads will take a day off your journey, and while there is every chance you will be stopped by patrols, you all speak better English than most of the men who may stop you. Keep your Irish in reserve. Remember you have as good a right to travel as anyone, but agree where you are going, why you are going, and why you are travelling alone. In that way, you will all give the same story if you're stopped. If Con can tie General Chichester in knots, you can.'

'Listen, now,' he continued, 'and I will give you the route you should follow.'

Sinéad listened, but her mind was still on her thoughtless whistle. *Perhaps Bonmann's saddling up to get me even now!*

'... then pick up the road to Newry,' Haystacks was explaining, 'but you must turn west before Slieve Gullion. There is a garrison at Castle Roche where you will certainly be stopped.'

Oh do be quick! Sinéad thought, anxious to be away.

'The Blackwater river will be your next hazard, as every crossing is guarded. I suggest you take the Blackwater fort, as it is a popular crossing. I'll ride the first miles with you, then you'll be on your own for a while. Remember, Con *must* be on that boat, or his life will be in danger. Come, we must go, before anyone else answers Sinéad's whistle.'

Fion cupped his hands to help Sinéad mount.

'Did you get all that?' she asked him.

'Oh yes,' he assured her. 'Don't forget, this is O'Neill country. I know it well.'

———⁂———

For the first few miles Haystacks led, followed by the others. They rode hard, but Sinéad kept dropping back, her eyes clasping at every familiar thing on the road: the broken-backed cottage where Eileen, the herbalist, lived, the oak they used to climb for mistletoe. *I may never see any of this again*, she kept reminding herself as tears welled up. She couldn't think of Mother or Father ... not yet ... but everything else was like crystal in her mind. When Haystacks slowed to keep her company, she managed a wan smile; he seemed to catch her sombre mood and they rode in silence. After a while she noticed his lips moving ever so slightly, and dared to ask him what he was thinking of.

'I was thinking of a poem, Sinéad. Long before the birth of Christ, a wandering prince came to Ireland. His name was Amergin, a Milesian they say. He left us with a poem which for me contains the essence of all poems. It begins like this, and he began to intone, half-speaking, half-singing:

> *I am the wind which breathes upon the sea,*
>
> *I am the wave of the ocean,*
>
> *I am the murmur of the billows ...*

After a short silence, Sinéad said: 'I like it, I like the sounds, I like what it makes me see. But is it the poet speaking or is it the wind and the wave?'

'Ha ha!' Haystacks laughed so loudly that the boys stopped and turned to see what was going on behind them. 'You shall be my apprentice, Sinéad – sorry – Brian. You have put your finger on the pulse of the matter. You see, the poet's task is to use his eyes, his ears and his heart until the wind blows through him, and the wave rises inside him, and they all become one – and then he can truly speak as a poet and say: *I am the wave of the ocean.*'

And then Haystacks recited the whole poem of Amergin, and for a while the terrible happenings of the past days fell away.

When he had finished, Sinéad's head felt clearer and she was ready to ride on.

'When we find Con, what then?' Sinéad shouted across to Haystacks. 'What will happen to *us*? We've got nothing now – no home, no money – and the only people who want us seem to want us dead.'

He didn't answer at once. When he did, he said: 'I wish I'd known your father better, Sinéad. He was a remarkable man. He knew that the safest thing for you to do was to escape from the castle, and he was prepared to trust you. "They are good children," he told me. "I trust them, but they'll need help." It was then that he asked me if I would go with you. I was already committed to helping Fion, so I agreed.' A sudden smile crossed Haystacks's face. 'I never thought I would acquire an apprentice for my pains.' Sinéad blushed. Then he said: 'There is more to tell you, but it is difficult to talk like this. I must leave you now as I have business to do. Fion knows your route; trust me – you'll be all right.'

***

Their road had been rising, and now broke free of the forest, and they could see Dundalk and the sea. They slowed to let the ponies catch their breath. Séamus, who had nicked his finger while trimming a hazel switch, stemmed the flow of blood with his kerchief.

'That's Slieve Gullion ahead,' Fion pointed out. 'I came near here when hunting for cattle that time for Uncle Hugh and your father, and beyond is Newry – and somewhere up there is Roche's Castle. Come on, let's go.'

As the road was now wide enough for conversation, Sinéad rode up between the two boys. She wanted to take their minds off the horrors they had all experienced. 'Haystacks was telling me about that castle as we came along,' she told them. 'It was built by a Norman lady called Rohesu to keep you wild Irish' – she glanced at Fion – 'under control. She had pots of money, but she couldn't get anyone to come up here into the wilds to build the castle for her. So, in the end, she offered herself in marriage to whoever would build her a castle. But they didn't exactly fall over themselves – she wasn't young, she was ugly as sin, and she had a fierce temper. Eventually, one brave architect, with more of an eye for her fortune than for herself, took up the offer and built her the Castle Roche, which Haystacks says means "castle on the rock" in French. Well, the marriage took place, and the feast was over, and they were climbing–' Here she had to break off as they had come to a crossroads.

'I think we should turn left here,' said Fion.

'Oh no, look, there are soldiers down there and coming this way. There'll be another turn surely,' said Séamus. 'Let's go on. You were telling us about the castle,' he added.

'So I was! Once up the stairs the not so lovely Rohesu leaned out of the bedchamber window, combing her hair – if she had any – and called to her new husband to come and take a close look at all the land he had got by marrying her. Poor soul, he came like a lamb and leaned out of the window beside her, whereupon she tipped him out and onto the rocks below, just to give him a closer look!'

'So, that was the end of him!'

'Oh no. You can see him any moonlit night standing in the bedchamber window – only it's bricked up now.'

They chuckled appreciatively, then Fion clapped his hand to his forehead, 'Which reminds me, have we got our story ready if we're stopped? You, Sinéad, or rather Brian, had better be Séamus's younger brother. I'll be a cousin, because I'm fair. So, why are we on the road, and where are we going?' They had only just settled on their story when they heard marching feet catching up with them from behind.

'Soldiers!' exclaimed Sinéad, looking over her shoulder. They urged their ponies on till they topped a gentle rise, and there, on the opposite side of a shallow valley, rose the towering walls of a castle, Castle Roche surely, perched like a panther ready to spring from its craggy outcrop. 'Now we're caught between the Devil and a rock!' This was no fortified house, but a proper fortress with a high curtain wall glinting with armed men. The red cross of St George flew from the keep and cooking smoke rose from hidden buildings within the walls.

'That's a long, long drop for a new husband!' said Sinéad in awe.

At that moment a voice roared out behind them: 'Hey there! Stand clear. You don't own the road!'

'We do actually – a lot more than you do!' snarled Fion under his breath, as they drew onto the verge. 'Now we're for it! It'll be us for the long drop!'

The column of soldiers ground to a halt. The officer, a brawny man with a drooping moustache, eyed their sturdy ponies and well-made harnesses.

'Well, now, what are you three lads roaming the country on your own for, eh? Running away? I'll bet your folk don't know where you are.'

'Oh yes, sir, they do, sir,' said Séamus in his best 'Fenton' English. 'They sent us away. We are to go to relatives in Newry, sir. They ... er ... er ... couldn't come.'

'Couldn't come? That's a bit lame. You'd better come with me to the castle and explain yourselves.' The three or four cavalry men who were attending the officer moved forward as if to take the reins from the children.

'Sir ... I think perhaps you shouldn't come close, sir. You see ...' and with this, Séamus appeared to catch his breath and he began a cough, which rapidly developed into a paroxysm of coughing which he tried to stifle with his kerchief. Sinéad and Fion watched in admiration as the fit shook him from head to toe. Suddenly, however, their admiration changed to alarm as he took the cloth away from his mouth to show it spattered scarlet with fresh blood! There was an audible gasp from the men, who drew back involuntarily.

Sinéad, who hadn't expected this extra bit of drama, had to gather her wits in a hurry, but now her rehearsed lines came to her rescue: 'Please, sir, please don't make him speak. You see, that's why we've been sent away. It's because ... of ... of ... the sickness at home.' She too, quite involuntarily, drew back at the sight of Séamus's bloody handkerchief. They'd talked of her bursting into tears, but she remembered just in time that 'Brian' would have died before weeping in front of the soldiers. The message, however, had got across and soldiers were already backing away.

'Plague, by God! I've got a hundred men in that castle, and you dare to come near us with the plague!' the officer accused them. 'It's the last thing we want! I should shoot you now, but then I'd have to bury your diseased corpses. No thanks. Go on to your family in Newry and give it to them if you must, but keep away from the castle.' He raised himself in his saddle. 'Sergeant! Quick – march!' And they set off as if they had a rabid dog at their heels.

'I only thought of the blood when I'd started coughing,' Séamus laughed. 'You see, I'd folded my kerchief bloody side in.' To his surprise, the others were almost cross with him at having scared them as well.

'All my horror wasted on a mere cut finger!' grumbled Sinéad. 'Let me look at it!' Séamus held it out. 'Pah! Don't expect any sympathy from me next time!'

All at once their eyes met, and with a splutter of delight they burst into laughter, the sound bouncing off the hills around.

At that precise moment, in the privacy of his old home, close under the reeking ruins of the de Cashel castle, Dr Henry Fenton was doing his best to persuade Sir Geoffrey Bonmann that he should chase after the children.

'But don't you see, Milord,' he squirmed, 'only the boy – James – stands between you and your claim to these lands through marriage to the girl. Get rid of him, get her – and it's all yours!'

'But there was no agweement with her father!'

Fenton's reply came as an exasperated whisper. 'So much the better! Wake up, man – we will *make up* an agreement. I wasn't de Cashel's secretary for nothing. But first we must find James.'

'And what will we do with him?'

'Leave that to me, Milord.'

'Perhaps I *should* mawwy the girl, after all ...'

'By all means!' said Fenton, thinking: *Over my dead body!* Once he had got rid of the boy and the girl there would be nobody to inquire about who had started the fire. Murder was easy to him now. *I must get this oaf away before he starts wondering who nearly fried him too.* 'Come, sir, we must go while their trail is warm.'

<hr>

The children were united now in their urgency. Hours passed in a routine of walking, trotting, galloping – and for backsides that were beginning to glow uncomfortably from hours in the saddle, welcome hills where they had to dismount and lead their tiring ponies. Eventually they reached a stream banked with fresh grass, where the ponies could graze and they could flop down and investigate their packs for food.

'A little and often is best,' said Séamus, quoting Father, as they inspected their rations.

'God bless Kathleen!' said Sinéad as she unwrapped a solid lump of mutton, as well as bread and hard cheese. Knowing Sinéad had no dagger, Kathleen had included a sharp knife, as well as a flint and steel and tinder to catch the spark if they needed a fire. *Typical! Dear Kathleen, I wonder if she's alive? I'll miss her terribly. Just think, when Kathleen packed this, Father and Mother were alive ... and now – STOP! I mustn't cry!*

They watched the ponies drinking, their mobile lips sucking at the water and listened for the swoosh of water inside their necks as they lifted their heads.

If it's good for them, it's good for us, they all agreed, and drank deeply from the stream themselves, cupping the water in their hands, and watching the scatter of diamond drops falling back onto the surface. They leaned back against their packs and closed their eyes and tried to relax, but their own private tragedies made it easier not to think, better to drive on.

They got through Armagh without challenge, and Fion told them how the remnants of Marshal Bagenal's army had gathered here after Uncle Hugh had beaten them at the Battle of the Yellow Ford only nine years before.

'Why do all the exciting things in history have to happen before my time?' Séamus complained.

'What d'you think this is?' snapped Sinéad.

⬥

With Armagh behind them, they had made great time, but their ponies were getting weary now, so they walked beside them more and more.

'We *must* cross the Blackwater before night, then it'll just be a sprint for the Sperrins in the morning,' urged Fion. 'We'll definietley find Con in time then.'

The thought of sprinting was almost too much for Sinéad as she eased herself into the saddle once more. But soon the ground levelled out, and across the meadows they could see trees that clearly flanked a river. Rising above the meadows, to the right of the road, were the earthworks and palisades of a fort, the cross of St George again showing it was in use. *Blackwater Fort*, Sinéad remembered.

A cart, piled high with wood for winter firing, lumbered towards them. The driver shouted across: 'Forget it, lads! They've closed the bloody bridge,' and he spat with disgust.

'Why? What's happening?' Séamus called.

'God knows. You'd think they'd seen the Devil himself walking on the water!' He cracked his whip and the cart lumbered on.

They met other travellers who had also been turned back, but none of them had any information. When they got to the bridge, they saw that a massive gate had been swung across to close it off. Soldiers from the fort were turning back anyone who approached. 'Only locals, and that's orders!'

'Well, what do we do now?' wondered Sinéad.

'Look, there's a path beside the river,' said Fion. 'Let's follow it. Try to look as if we know where we're going. Maybe we'll find somewhere where we can hole up for the night and get some hay for the ponies.'

After a quarter of a mile or so they did find a cottage with a barn, where they were told they might sleep, and, for a halfpenny, buy hay and a bag of oats for the ponies. They were worn out, so after a sparse supper there seemed to be nothing to do but settle for the night.

Séamus, however, was restless. 'Do you think Haystacks will be looking for us? I'm going to wander back to the bridge in case he's following us.' But what he really needed was somewhere to think, so he turned up-river to where a narrow path led down through the reeds to a little wooden jetty. There was a boat there, sunk to its gunwales, half-hidden in the reeds. It looked a wreck, but the rope that tied it to the jetty was new. He sat down. An otter appeared on the bank below him, looked upstream, then down, called once and slid into the water, where it rolled on its back to watch its three full-grown kits slip in to join it. Only that morning, Séamus realised, he had been pinning his hopes on Chichester. *How did I let myself be so fooled by Fenton? Of course my loyalty must be to Uncle Hugh now! If we don't find Con, and the English do, they'll hold him hostage until Uncle Hugh surrenders. I need to prove my loyalty, and the best way to do that is to find Con.*

The light was fading fast when he reached the bridge where the soldiers had lit torches and a brazier to keep warm. He tried them in English first, but soon found that they were Irish conscripts, so it wasn't long before he was holding his hands out to the brazier, happily talking about army life. After a bit, he thought it safe to ask why they were blocking the bridge. 'It's not falling down on us, is it?'

They laughed, but they dropped their voices. 'A constable in the village reported seeing a party of well-dressed travellers passing through late last night, and some idiot started a rumour that it was the Earl of Tyrone! Bloody nonsense. Everyone here knows he's off to London in chains to have the head eased from his shoulders. Anyway, they want the bridge closed – maybe they think there's more rebels on the road.'

For a while now, Séamus had been aware of the sound of

approaching hooves. *Haystacks,* he thought hopefully, but this was a whole group of horsemen.

The soldiers were listening too. 'Here comes the Earl and all his ladies!' one of them joked. Séamus backed away into the darkness. He should leave, but he was curious. It was a group of five horsemen: three men at arms behind two vaguely familiar figures on horseback.

'Halt, sir! The bridge is closed,' the sergeant called out.

'Let me pass, soldier. I'm on important business for Milord Chichester.'

'I'm a sergeant, I'll thank'y, sir, and who's that with you?'

'It's my secwetawy,' said the voice.

Séamus could have been struck by lightning. *Bonmann! And Fenton with him. What are they doing here?* He didn't have to wait for his answer.

'Seen three youngsters on ponies? Did they pass here?'

Séamus shuffled back, ready to run, but the sergeant, clearly narked at Bonmann's lordly manner, snapped out: 'We're not here to police children – *sir*. The bridge is closed. If you want to pass, you can report to the fort's commander!'

'I will – and I'll weport you to the commander for insolence!' At that they wheeled off and up the slope to the entrance of the fortress.

Séamus wanted to thank the sergeant, but instead he continued to edge back out of the light, then turned and ran hell-for-leather down the path. The moon hadn't risen yet, so it was pitch dark as he turned off the path towards the barn, only to collide with something huge; a horse tethered beside the door snorted with indignation. Heart hammering, he heaved at the barn door.

He expected Fion and Sinéad to be asleep, but they were sitting up, mirror images on each side of a single candle.

'They're after us,' he blurted out. 'Bonmann and Fenton with three men at arms. If only Haystacks were here!'

'Oh but he is!' declared a deep voice from the shadows. Once again, Séamus nearly jumped out of his skin: *Haystacks!* 'Come on, Séamus, tell us what you know!' and Haystacks emerged from the shadows.

Putting his own questions to one side, Séamus told them about the soldiers on the bridge, and the horsemen.

'Are you sure?' Fion asked.

'Oh yes.' Séamus had no doubts.

'I was afraid of this,' declared Haystacks. 'Bonmann thinks that you, Séamus, are the only obstacle to his claiming your lands. Fenton has your parents' murder on his conscience and won't sleep easy until he has both you and Sinéad out of his way. You have dangerous enemies.'

'I don't think the sergeant on the bridge will link me to three missing children, and anyway he clearly disliked Bonmann,' said Séamus.

'Perhaps,' agreed Haystacks, 'but the chances are, someone saw you when you turned along the river. We can expect visitors. We must be gone by first light, but to where?' Haystacks scratched his head. 'Every regular crossing on the Blackwater will be guarded.'

Séamus leapt to his feet. 'Haystacks! I've got it. I didn't pass you on your way here because I was down by the river – and there's a boat there, submerged in the water, but the rope that holds it is new. Come, I'll show you. My guess is that the owner sank it on purpose to keep it hidden – maybe he does a little smuggling on the side. If we bail it out, I think we can get ourselves and the gear across. Our ponies have all swum before.'

They left immediately as none of them could even think of sleeping.

***

Sinéad would remember the crossing of the Blackwater as a night of misery. The boat could only take two at a time, so she found herself dumped on a small jetty on the far side of the river pulling on a rope while the boys tried to persuade the ponies, one after the other, to take to the water and swim across. Eventually they were all over, splashed and frozen, trying to load their shivering mounts with deadened fingers.

The smuggler's path by-passed the village on the far side of the river so they were able to join the road well away from its dangers and settle down to cover the miles.

Haystacks, having some mission of his own, said he would catch them up later.

CHAPTER 17

Crab Apples
and the Search for Con

on steered Macha down the side of the valley to where the Glenelly river sliced the Sperrin mountains in two. One time he'd found a pebble in the river here, bright with flecks of gold; he still carried it in a pouch about his neck for luck. September had arrived and these were the last days he'd have free in the mountains, his last opportunity for any sort of adventure, so he would make the most of it.

He gave Macha a slap with his hand and was off up the hill. Half an hour later he was clear of the forest, letting his pony zigzag up the mountainside more or less as he liked. The front of Con's shirt bulged with small crab-apples that he had picked, reaching from his saddle, a little down the slope. His cattle pole, now tucked under his knee, stuck out in front like a lance.

Each spring his foster family, the O'Brolchains, would drive the cattle entrusted to their care by Hugh O'Neill and others up to the summer pastures on the Sperrin mountains. There they would have grass enough to thrive, and by their absence allow the cutting of hay and sowing of crops in the lowlands. Then, in autumn, the herdsmen would bring the cattle down to the warmer land below. As he climbed from the valley, the oak, the ash and the alder gave way to scattered pines, and finally to grass and heather. This was Con's kingdom – and he decided not to think about the dreary months ahead minding the cattle in their corrals. Down there the air would be as thick as soup, and the ground a sea of liquid dung. He whistled quietly to himself.

That summer he had had two whole months with his father, Hugh O'Neill. 'I'm pinning my hopes on you, Con,' his father had told him. 'You see, I too was a rascal horse-boy once, just like you. We're peas from the same pod, you and I. One day we will make waves and they had all better watch out!' Now, however, something was disturbing Con's thoughts; it was a scent on the air. He whispered to Macha to stand still, and he sniffed. There! The scent of burning wood and something else that was tantalising – he couldn't decide what it was. Now, who was up here lighting a fire? Interesting. He tested the breeze and nudged Macha to move up-wind in that direction. There was a concealed valley here, a mere wrinkle in the hillside ahead. He slid out of his saddle, dropped the reins to tell Macha to stand, and moved towards the valley rim. Then he crouched, and finally crawled on his hands and knees to the edge. There was a rowan tree there that offered cover. It was a pretty tree, its green crown jewelled with scarlet berries, but Con was more interested in what he was seeing below.

There were five of them, English soldiers for certain – two of them officers, at a guess. They looked very comfortable down there beside the stream. They had a small tent – for the officers, no doubt – a camp-fire and a pan and ... aaah! ... bliss! there it was, the smell of bacon frying.

Con knew what he should do – slink away unseen and tell the drovers, who would pass the word on. Then, in a little while, five new horses, a couple of muskets and a fine sword or two would be passed around in their camp, and there would be five new graves somewhere in the forest. The English never seemed to learn how easy it was to wander into Irish territory, and how difficult it was to leave it. Con felt a sudden empathy with these men. They were cheeky, just like him. He would tease them a bit. He reached into his shirt, felt for an apple, then threw it with remarkable accuracy and hit one of the officers on the back.

'Hey! What was that?' The officer spun about, then spotted the apple and looked up as if expecting to see an apple tree suddenly grown above him. He turned to the soldiers. 'Come on! Which of you threw that?'

'I didn't!'

'You did!'

'It must have been one of you!'

'Not us, sir!'

'Yes, it damn well was!'

Con was in stitches. This was better than he could have imagined – and all with one small apple. He threw another and started them off again.

'You did!'

'I didn't!'

He threw a third apple, but didn't wait to see where it landed when he heard shouts of: 'Up there ... that bush ... where's my pistol?'

He was still nearly doubled with laughter when he arrived back to Macha, who was nibbling at the heather fifty yards away. But he had to think quickly now. The soldiers had horses and one or more of them might have a loaded musket. The sensible thing was for him to run for it – they'd hardly bother to hunt down a mere boy – but when Con had the devil in him, sense was not a high priority. He tore off his shirt, scattering crab-apples like musket balls about him. Then he used its long sleeves to tie it to his cattle pole and raised it, a brilliant yellow flag above his head, and rode towards the valley rim. Taking a deep breath he stuck two fingers in his mouth and gave his loudest ever wolf-whistle. He'd been practising his piercing whistle ever since he'd been shown it by that girl from de Cashel's castle. He stopped short of the valley rim, hoping that his flag would be visible from below, and whistled again; then he cantered along the rim just out of sight. Whenever he could, he whistled high or low as the mood took him, as if mustering a large group of men for a charge. Any doubt about them seeing him was dispelled when a musket ball hissed past his flag, followed almost instantly by a blast of the gun. Now was the time for him to clear out. They'd be upon him in a minute, but he couldn't resist a quick look. He looked, and then he looked again, because they were gone: tent, horses, cooking pots and all. He could see the last of them disappearing down the slope. Bemused at his success, he rode cautiously down. No, it wasn't a trap. The fire was still burning, and out of habit he dismounted in order to quench the flames and cover the ashes. Then the breeze from the fire wafted in his direction. He sniffed ... and sniffed again. His stomach growled, his mouth watered – bacon! He dropped to his knees beside the fire; there in the embers were the rashers that the army scouts must have tipped out of the pan as they ran. They were still bubbling and hissing – covered in ashes, certainly, but who minded ashes? *The spoils of war,* Con thought, as he fell on them.

After Haystacks had left them, Séamus took over the lead, fired with enthusiasm, and Fion rode beside Sinéad. 'Well, we've got to hand it to Séamus,' he said, 'that river-crossing was brilliant.'

She smiled, glad for her brother. 'He has a new cause now, Fion. God help poor England!' she chuckled.

Fion nodded. 'Just think, but for him, you might be breakfasting with your future husband, and we'd probably be in chains.'

'I know. But what will happen to us here in Ireland, Fion, when

Uncle Hugh has gone?' She gazed about at the untended land. Everywhere were traces of past farming activity, but now burned and tumbled homesteads were all that was left, the land overtaken by weeds and encroaching forest.

'This is Mountjoy's work, though Chichester did most of it for him,' said Fion. 'This country used to be rich and peaceable – they talk of herds of cattle, a hundred thousand strong, and of farmsteads set in gold from the wheat, barley and oats around them. Apart from the occasional cattle raid, there was peace and harmony here. We didn't need to be instructed by the English in civilisation. Haystacks could have walked from here to Donegal with only a staff against dogs; he'd have been fed in every home, welcomed by every chief and child, and if anything went amiss, he'd have been protected by our own Brehon laws.'

'Do you think the English really want to civilise us, Fion?'

'No, Sinéad, make no mistake, they want just one thing: they want *land* – your land, my land, our land. When they took Uncle Hugh and fostered him in England, they wanted to turn him into a gentleman, not out of love, but because if he became English they'd have their hands on half of Ulster. Look how they reward their generals! They give them land, not because they like their generals, but because each one will hold that bit of Ireland for King James and England.'

'Ireland's ruined now!' she said sadly.

'The land will recover, but the people won't. When Mountjoy found he couldn't trap Uncle Hugh, he gave Chichester licence to do what he chose. Whole villages were burned – men, women and children chopped to pieces – but it wasn't swords and pikes that emptied the land, but hunger. When the soldiers came we could escape into the forests, but our crops and our cattle couldn't, so the English took what they could and destroyed the rest. My old nurse – from before I was fostered with you – loved to scare me with stories of what was happening. I still have a nightmare in which I am walking down a road like this. Each side is a ditch full of human half-skeletons their mouths open, all waving claw-like hands at me. As I walk, the road gets narrower and narrower until the hands are brushing me; finally they clutch my legs and I can't move. I stop and I look down. Their mouths are wide open like baby birds demanding to be fed, and I can see that inside they are stained with the green juice from nettles and grass they have been chewing. And the people who had created this famine threw up their hands and called us savages.'

'Look, that must be Dungannon ahead,' said Sinéad, relieved to change the subject.

Haystacks joined them just as they emerged from the town.

'You look pleased,' commented Fion when he rode up.

Haystacks chuckled. 'For the moment, yes. I don't like the role of informer, but I thought it was only fair to write a polite note to Sir Geoffrey Bonmann and inform him, firstly that the fire in the castle had been deliberate, and secondly that it had been started by one of the party he now had with him.'

'Fenton!'

'Precisely. But I thought we might win ourselves a little time if he had to work that out for himself. Who knows how it will help us. At best we will have brought a murderer to justice.'

'And you signed this letter?'

'Of course! Nobody believes an anonymous letter,' he said indignantly, then grinned, 'I signed it "Mr Haystacks".'

All day they rode north-west. Behind them the leaden waters of Lough Neagh receded into the distance. The air was sultry, the calm before the storm, perhaps. At one point exhaustion hit Sinéad like a lead weight and the temptation to roll from the saddle, lie in the grass and just sleep … slee …

'Watch out, Sinéad!' and she felt Fion's grip on her arm as he pulled her up straight in her saddle.

Haystacks and Fion kept asking any passersby for news of the O'Brolchains. Sometimes they were greeted cheerily, sometimes with suspicion. 'Did you see how that fellow kept fiddling with my harness?' asked Fion once in annoyance. 'He was calculating what it was worth, I reckon.'

'What you're worth, more likely,' said Haystacks. 'Ever since O'Cahan went over to the English, and Chichester put a bounty on your uncle's head, his hangers-on have been looking for rewards for themselves. Come on, here are the mountains.'

Sinéad looked ahead to where the mountains were shouldering themselves above the trees; it seemed a vast area in which to find one small boy. Her heart sank when Haystacks said again: 'I will leave you now, I must ride northwards. The country up there is less faithful to Tyrone, but Con could still be there.'

They rode in single file, their ponies' hooves pattering on an almost deserted road. The setting sun lit up the bases of lowering storm clouds. Rain threatened and they had no shelter and nowhere to rest their heads.

Yet another stop, and Sinéad leaned her face into her pony's mane and began to cry.

'Hey, Sinéad,' called Fion a short while later. 'Wake up. Success at last!' She struggled upright. Fion had a lanky seventeen-year-old beside him. 'Micheál here tells me the O'Brolchain camp is just over that ridge. They're bringing the cattle down from the high ground for the winter – he's going there to help, and will guide us over. Wake up, girl, we've found Con! Micheál saw him only last week!'

But Sinéad was looking at the mountain. 'How are we going to get over that?' she wailed.

Fion laughed. 'Micheál says there's a pass between the mountains that we can follow; it's tricky to find, but he's going to show us the way.'

As if sharing their relief, the ponies pricked their ears and followed willingly as their new friend plunged off the road to follow a zigzag path up through the trees cloaking the valley side. Micheál strode ahead on foot, waiting when the tired ponies began to dip their heads into the climb. They rose out of the oak woods just as dusk was falling. Above them towered the mountain. Then, quite suddenly, the hillside seemed to open in front of them and there was the path, winding into the hill between steep bluffs and craggy outcrops of rock. Ferns sprang up from the wet banks in green fountains, catching the last of the light and making it their own. Now the path was plunging down and Sinéad, leaning back, had to push her feet forward in her stirrups to stop herself sliding over her pony's head. The stream, which had started as a trickle, now chattered to them cheerily. For a moment Sinéad looked out over the forest canopy that filled the valley like a rolling sea, then they plunged down into it, and the trees closed protectively over their heads.

A new quiet settled over the party, their ponies' hooves suddenly hushed in leaf litter from thousand-year-old trees. Before they realised that they had arrived, they found themselves surrounded by sloping tents and thatched shelters, all in a pleasant haze of woodsmoke. This was the O'Brolchain winter camp. Women and children crowded out to see the new arrivals; the men were away on the mountain to gather the cattle. Sinéad sat in her saddle, swaying with tiredness, until she found herself looking down at a girl of about Con's age.

'I'm Aoife, but you don't look like a Brian,' said the girl seriously. Sinéad smiled; she'd been sussed already, but it would be a relief to be a girl again, and to be with another girl, even a small and grubby one. When Micheál came offering to take her pony to rub her dow...

hall in which t...

men. She thought si...

duced a bowl of thick, stea...

stomach. Neither of them said a...

was empty and she sat back with a sigh.

'Why are you here?' asked the girl suspiciou...

'We have come to find Con and bring him to his ...

'Oh!' said the girl – then defiantly, 'Good riddance!'

Sinéad wasn't fooled, but at that moment the boys bounced in.

'Well, we've found him!' Fion crowed.

'He'll be down from the mountain at first light,' said Séamus, 'and then we've just got to get him to the sh–'

He stopped. Aoife was taking in every word. Haystacks had insisted: No mention of the ship, even to Sean O'Brolchain himself.

'This is Aoife,' said Sinéad, hurriedly introducing the young girl, who tossed her head and marched away, but came back in a minute with two man-sized bowls of stew for the boys. She thumped them down on the table, and walked out.

'What's the matter with her?' Séamus asked, but forgot about it with his first spoonful. 'Wow, what a stew!'

———

That night Sinéad lay under her cloak on a huge communal bed in the women's tent; the wind was soughing in the treetops far above.

...nd of rain drumming on the

...we're not out in that! she thought. She

...then that Aoife had slipped in beside her. It was the first proper sleep Sinéad had had for several days.

However, Con didn't arrive at first light; in fact, he didn't come at all.

<hr />

That very night Henry Fenton looked out from his prison cell at the noose of the gallows swinging in the wind. He rubbed his neck as if the rope was already closing about him. *Curse whoever wrote that note!* he thought. *What damnable luck, one of Bonmann's men seeing me with the torch before I lit the fire in the castle.* For all his lawyer's cleverness, Fenton had had no defence. It was a military court, and his sentence, 'death by hanging', was to take place at first light. *Oh, the sight of the gallows!* He wiped the sweat from his forehead. *Think!*

Before that hateful note had arrived, the fortress had been alive with rumours. Now, piece by piece, he put the rumours together: *O'Neill is clearly on the move, gathering his wife, Catherine, and their sons together like chickens; it must be a family gathering. Something important is happening ... perhaps someone is coming ... an army? ... an ambassador? ... surely that's it ... but no ... you don't gather your family for an ambassador nor yet a general. Think, you fool! Why the family? ... why ... holy smoke!* Fenton leapt to his feet. *I've got it! It's not someone coming it's someone going. Jesus, Mary, and Joseph:*

Hugh O'Neill's fleeing!

'Guard!' he yelled. 'Send word to Sir Geoffrey Bonmann that I have information for him that will change his life.'

The guard grumbled off.

Now, before he comes, how do I play my cards? Hints ... enough to keep me from the gallows! Then bluff ... he must think that I know where the boat will sail from – we'll find those kids and make damn sure they show us.

There was a jangle of keys.

'Dwat the man! What does he want to confess? I'm not a pwiest.'

No, but you are a fool, thought Fenton. Then he laid out his baits: *the Earl of Tyrone to be captured in flight, sundry lords and ladies as well, rewards and glory for Bonmann, and, as if that was not enough, once he had disposed of the de Cashel children, there would be no one to stop him claiming their castle lands for himself. That should do the trick!* thought Fenton. And it did.

<hr />

There was pandemonium in the O'Brolchain camp. The autumn cattle drive was underway, soon the pens would be full of lowing beasts, and Con had gone missing!

'I'll skin that lad when I get him,' roared Sean O'Brolchain, tearing at his hair. 'What does Hugh O'Neill want him for, anyway?'

Nevertheless, men were diverted to search for him. Fion and

Séamus rode out to join the search, but they dared not go far in case Con suddenly appeared. Minutes, and then hours passed without a sign. When Haystacks rode in, confident that they were all well on their way, he found them kicking their heels beside their saddled ponies.

'What on earth are you waiting for? It will soon be dark!' he exclaimed. So Fion had to explain how they had been looking for Con all day.

Haystacks thought long and hard. 'After all this, to fail!' he said with a sigh. 'There is only one thing to do and that is get word to Lord O'Neill that Con is missing; the boat must not be delayed. You, Fion, must leave anyway; and Séamus and Sinéad have no home to go to and are in danger from Bonmann and Fenton – perhaps there will be room for the three of you on the boat. We'll give Con an hour, then you must leave. I will wait. If Con appears, I'll follow. Surely *someone* knows where he's hiding.'

Con O'Neill wasn't hiding, he was sitting on his pony on the summit of Sawel mountain looking down on the O'Cahan herd below. All summer he had wanted to ride up here, to where Tyrone country and O'Cahan country met, but he hadn't been allowed. 'I bet they'll be gathering their cattle up there now,' he had told Aoife. 'Don't tell a soul, but I think they owe us a cow, the traitors.'

'Macha, *a chroí*, we may have to run for it,' he murmured now to his pony as he tried to decide on which animal to single out. 'You see that young heifer there that's wandering up in our direction? We'll round her up. If we get her into Tyrone territory, I win; but if we don't – I lose, and I'll forfeit my gold pebble to Aoife to stop her plaguing me for it. Let's go!' Cattle pole at the ready, he trotted forward.

O'Cahan's herdsmen were strangely slow to spot the one-boy cattle-raid that was taking place under their noses. Con circled the heifer without being noticed and was now making good progress up the hill. Just a hundred yards more and they would be over the summit, into Tyrone territory, and that would be one in the eye for the O'Cahans. At that moment, however, there came a roar of rage from the herdsmen below.

'This is it, Macha! Seventy yards more.' He could hear horses' hooves closing on him. Fifty yards. 'Come on, my darling!' he shouted at the heifer. Twenty-five yards; the top of the hill was close, but the heifer was slowing. It had never occurred to Con that they might shoot at him, but it was the bang of a pistol that won the race for him. Whether or not the bullet had actually stung the heifer he would never know, but with a toss of her head and a kick of her heels she was off and over the top into Tyrone territory before he could blink.

Amazingly, his pursuers stopped at the border – perhaps they suspected a trick – but Con kept going until he was out of range of their pistols. Then he turned, doffed an imaginary hat, and gave the heifer a slap on the rump that sent it back home. His point had been made. He then rode off with all the dignity he could muster; he was already rehearsing a colourful version of the tale for Aoife.

———❦———

Sinéad went to find the girl. *I bet she knows where Con is, but how do I get her to tell?* Sinéad imagined that she was Aoife: *I'll stick by Con no matter what – I know where he is, but I swore not to tell anyone, least of all these bossy children who want to take him away.*

As she'd guessed, Sinéad was met with a clamped jaw and shuttered eyes. But she was imagining herself as Aoife now, loyal to her small heart's core, and in that moment knew that only one thing would unlock her mind – and that was the truth. It was a monumental risk, but she knew now that Aoife would guard their secret as if it were Con's once she knew why. So Sinéad told her everything: about the ship, the waiting Earl, and the danger to Con. Little by little the shutters lifted and Aoife began to tell her about Con, until finally ... finally, she told Sinéad where Con was. When Sinéad gave Aoife a final hug, the child was as stiff as a board again; not even torture would get a word of O'Neill's flight out of her now.

———❦———

Keeping to the ridge, Con followed it west; his planned route was to cross the valley directly opposite the O'Brolchain camp. The wind was still strong, and a blast of rain momentarily blanked out any view further than the few yards of heather ahead of him. He pulled his hooded cloak over his head and bent into the rain. It cleared almost as soon as it had come; he raised his head, and pulled Macha to a halt. *Who on God's earth are those? One, two, three ponies and a man, in my territory; I can't leave them unchallenged.* Lowering his cattle pole like a lance, he whistled a loud challenge and charged down the slope towards them.

⸺⸺

Sinéad's heart was sinking. There was still no sign of Con, and they were up in the mountains wasting time. Rain lashed at them. Then suddenly, from high above them, came a piercing whistle. They looked up, and there, flying down the ridge at them, holding his cattle pole as if to run them through, came a boy on a pony.

'Con!' they exclaimed as one.

Sinéad put her two fingers in her mouth and gave her own challenging whistle. That brought the boy's head up. He seemed to be having second thoughts about running them all through, and raised his pole in the air. Ignoring Haystacks, he rode up to challenge the children.

'Which one of you whistled?' he demanded.

'Me! The person who taught you how to whistle yourself, Con O'Neill, son of Hugh. Don't you recognise a lady when you see one?'

Con's bewilderment was comic, a mixture of bluster and apology, first that the smaller of the boys was a girl, and then to recognise her as the girl who had indeed taught him to whistle. They all dismounted. When Con recognised Haystacks as the man who had helped him through the plashing, he became almost polite. But this was no time for lengthy explanations.

Fion formally delivered Hugh O'Neill's command for Con to join him on his ship at Rathmullan no later than tomorrow evening. Con's expression changed from disbelief to consternation, and then to delight as Haystacks told him what this meant. 'New adventure' was written all over the boy's face. Haystacks then said: 'We have very little time, and you will want to collect clothes for the journey, and make your farewells.'

Clothes? Farewells? Nonsense! 'But I can come now, as long as I have Macha to carry me,' he said airily. 'I don't need anything.'

'Good,' said Haystacks, 'but we must get word to your foster family that you have been found; you will want me to greet them on your behalf.'

'Oh it doesn't matter – the O'Brolchains are just herdsmen, you know.'

Sinéad gasped. *You arrogant little prig! You may not care for them, but they care for you!* 'Herdsmen or not,' she said tartly, 'there is someone there who admires you more than you will ever deserve. Have you nothing, no token, no keepsake for her? She knows what loyalty means, even if you don't!'

For a second or two Con pretended he hadn't understood what Sinéad was saying. Then he dropped his eyes. 'There's Aoife, of course,' he said. There was a long pause while Con remembered that he had won the bet over the heifer ... Finally, reluctantly, he reached inside his shirt, pulled out a small leather pouch, and extracted a pebble from it.

'This is for Aoife, so,' he shrugged, 'a keepsake.' He dropped it onto Haystacks's palm. They all bent forward to look. At first glance it appeared to be just an ordinary water-worn pebble, but as Haystacks turned it over, bright flecks and ribbons of real gold flashed from its surface.

'It's heavy,' murmured Haystacks.

'Here, take this too,' Con handed him the pouch, 'else she'll only lose it.' *Well done!* thought Sinéad. Con then gave Haystacks a gracious message of thanks for the O'Brolchains.

Haystacks turned away. 'I'll catch you up,' he said. 'You'll be easily followed – and I hope it's just me that will be following.'

***

'Dwat them anyway!' exclaimed Bonmann. 'This is the second time we've been given wong diwections!'

'That's because you treat them like dirt,' said Dr Fenton. 'Next time, you stand back and I'll ask in Irish!' *Pity they haven't put a spear through you already,* he thought.

***

Con managed to look superior for about a mile, riding beside the others as if they were low company. *Damned girl, dressed up as a boy ... how was I to know!* Then he thought of Sean and Maire

O'Brolchain – kind but tough – who beat him as regularly as they beat their dogs, which wasn't often, but always well deserved. He blushed. *I didn't really mean it about them being just herdsmen.* He looked up at the receding mountain, not wanting the others to read his thoughts. Then he thought of Aoife and a sudden lump formed in his throat. *But I did give her my pebble,* he thought, *and she's wanted it since the day I found it.* Gradually he felt better about himself and able to think about what was happening. *I can't believe it – going with Father on a ship to Spain! How do they know about this plan and how did they know where to find me?* He looked across at the two boys. He was not normally bothered by people older than himself, but he was still feeling a little bit small. Then he remembered the boy/girl's name, Sinéad. She'd looked like a proper girl then and had surprised the life out of him by whistling like Father. Better than that, she'd taught him how to do it too. Perhaps she'd tell him more about Father's message; he pulled Macha over to her side. It was not long before he was entertaining her with tales of his recent adventures in the mountains.

Light was fading fast when they reached the river Foyle. Con respected his companions now. They could ride like demons; but Macha had had a day on the hills, while their ponies were rested. They halted and watched people plodding homeward after a day at the market. There was a patrol stopping people and looking into their bags and baskets. Was this normal? Were the soldiers extra vigilant?

'I think we should split up and attach ourselves to different groups,' Fion said. 'Look, Con, see that woman with a bundle of sticks, why don't you offer your pony to help her with them over the bridge? We'll meet up at the next turn after the bridge.' They watched while Con charmed a toothless smile from the old woman, and then gave her an arm as he led his pony straight past the soldiers and across the bridge. Fion quietly hitched his pony to the back of a laden cart without the owner noticing, and then walked across with a group of apprentices from the tannery. They stank from their work, and were waved through quickly, as they laughed at the soldier who was holding his nose. Fion was relieved to find his pony still behind the cart when it caught up with them.

'You're grubby enough to be a serving boy, Sinéad,' said Séamus. 'Why don't you lead the ponies while I ride,' he suggested.

'Pah!' said Sinéad, taking the reins and slouching across the bridge in front of her 'young master'. 'You'll pay for this!' she warned.

When they were all safely across, Fion took the lead again. 'We've got to press on. If we do, we should reach Rathmullan early tomorrow, let's go!' When they got to the village of Ballindrait they paused to ask the way of a garrulous old man at the bridge. 'You'd best be quick, my little lords, if it's Milord O'Neill you want. He's a good hour ahead of you – he with his lady, and our own chief, Caffar O'Donnell.'

'Which road did they take?'

'The Letterkenny road,' and the old man winced as he pointed. 'Me joints is all seized up,' he complained.

'If Caffar O'Donnell's your chief, and if you are true to Ireland and Hugh O'Neill, you'll tell no one that you saw them on the road tonight,' said Fion, handing him sixpence, a handsome reward for silence. At that, they spurred their ponies over the bridge. 'We must keep going – they could sail the moment they reach the ship, Con or no Con. Come on!' Fion urged.

Soon, however, they slowed to a more sensible pace, reminding themselves that they still had many miles to go. They were followed by a fleeting moon as they rode through the night. It was still dark when the road dipped down to cross the Swilly river just short of Letterkenny. The town gates were just being opened by sleepy-looking guards.

'Well,' said Fion, 'no sign of Uncle Hugh. Either they got through before the gates closed or they have taken another route.'

'Oh come on!' urged Con. 'The boat may be sailing now.'

'We must be careful!' said Fion.

'Rot!' said Con. 'You're wimps, the lot of you. If we take it at a gallop, they're so dopey we'll be through and gone while they're still scratching their backsides.'

At that moment there was a flash, a spurt of smoke, and a boom from the guard post beside the gate. The children ducked instinctively, but no ball whistled past.

'What was that?' exclaimed Con.

'One them scratching his backside, I suspect,' said Fion acidly. A man came out of the guard-post, stretching. 'I think it was just the signal to say that the gates are open now. Let's be sensible for a change, Con. Séamus, why don't you ride ahead, followed by Sinéad, but riding far enough back to give Con and me warning if Séamus is stopped. I bet Uncle Hugh took some other route – I wish we had now.'

Séamus called out to the guards that they'd been out hunting, and they trooped through. Sinéad held back as Séamus went ahead.

Séamus was just thinking that they would be through without trouble when a figure lurched towards him and grabbed his pony's bridle. His first thought was to lash out with his reins, but then he realised that this wasn't an attack. He looked down. There in the centre of a mass of bristles – hair, eyebrows, beard, it was hard to say – were two red-rimmed eyes.

'God help me. Ye must be Red Hugh O'Donnell ris' up from the grave,' said the man, swaying, and using the bridle for support. 'Had black hair, you know ... just like you. Betrayed he was by that red-haired Tyrone man, O'Neill, down at Kin... Kinwhatever... the swine.' Séamus thought of Con's hair, like a flaming torch, behind. He groped for a coin, extracted it, and – oops! – he'd dropped it! Down went the beggar on hands and knees, letting go of the bridle, and Séamus rode on. The beggar was still groping as the others trotted hastily by.

The road rose steeply out of the town so they had to walk the ponies for a mile or two, and were just about to mount when Fion held up a hand. 'Listen! We're being followed!'

Sure enough, they all heard it now: a horse's hooves.

CHAPTER 18

The Flight of the Earls

aystacks nearly missed them, huddled in the mouth of a lane. Séamus told him about the incident with the beggar. 'Did Red Hugh really have black hair?' he asked.

'He did indeed,' chuckled Haystacks. 'More to the point, how much did you drop for him, Séamus?'

Séamus looked sheepish. 'It was the only coin I could put my hand on – a shilling, I think!' The others gasped.

'That explains it. That will be the beggar I met in the town singing his heart out and carrying the biggest bottle of poteen I've ever seen.' They had to laugh. He changed the subject, 'No sign of the Earl's party?'

'We nearly caught up with them in a place called Ballindrait,' said Fion. 'But we think they must have gone some other way; the town gates were only just opening when we came through.'

'Right, we must press on. It's likely the Earl's ship will sail the moment he's on board.'

At Rathmelton, Haystacks found that his horse had a loose shoe, so they were forced to take rest while he went to find a smithy. It was a chance to finish the food Maire O'Brolchain had provided for them.

Con was too excited to eat. *Come on, come on,* he urged in his mind, imagining a triumphal arrival at the head of his small troop; *pity one of them has to be a girl, but at least she doesn't look like one.* First Father'd give him a cuff on the ear for being late, then there'd be the bear-like hug. He imagined the ship at a quay-side, ready to sail, its rail lined by courtly nobles, while local chieftains in saffron would be kneeling for their departing lord. Pipes would play–

'Come on, Con, aren't you coming?' called Haystacks, and Con was jerked out of his reverie. 'We're nearly there. We've as good as made it, boy.'

After the steep climb out of the village they took advantage of every flat or downward slope to trot, or even canter. The sky had cleared, and the air was washed clean by the storm. Sinéad kept glancing at the sea, which, borrowing blue from the sky, flashed like a kingfisher in flight. At last, Haystacks gave a shout and pointed ahead. There, her sails unfurled and ready to be turned to the wind, rode a ship, the flag of France floating in the light wind. As they pulled up, their tiredness fell away. Five days in the saddle and they had arrived at last.

'But it's French!' said Sinéad.

'Yes, but it's going to Spain,' explained Haystacks.

'Look, they're ready to sail!' shouted Con, as he whammed his feet into Macha's sides, who, catching his mood, responded like a pent-up spring.

'Stop, Con! Stop! We must be careful!' called Haystacks, but Con was gone, and the others, who could see nothing to be careful about either, took off after him, whooping with excitement.

Haystacks held back. *They deserve to let their hair down,* he thought, but he was worried. The road dipped to pass across a tree-lined valley, and he could see the children, racing each other now, as they disappeared from view under the trees. He stood in his stirrups, counting seconds, staring at the point where their road emerged from the trees at the other side. They should be appearing – now! But nothing moved. What could have happened? A hundred yards beyond the trees and they would be in sight of the boat and safe. His horse fretted, longing to join the race, but Haystacks held him back. Why had they not appeared? A sick feeling formed in his stomach – *over all these miles trying to anticipate everything that might go wrong, and here we are at the very end! What can have happened? Could one of them have fallen? There!* A whistle somewhere below. *Con's? Sinéad's?* He gathered his reins; it was clearly a call for help!

He was just about to hurtle after them when a horseman appeared on the road facing him. The man stopped, looked in his direction, and turned to wave to someone behind him. Now the man was urging his horse up the hill. This was no welcome; it was a pursuit, but still Haystacks lingered. What had happened to the children? A glance over his shoulder – there were two after him now. A puff of smoke and the whiz of a bullet decided things for him. He turned, laid himself low on his horse's back and galloped away. He never carried arms, and there was nothing he could do for his young charges at this moment apart from getting away from his pursuers. But Haystacks had many skills, and making himself invisible in rough country was one.

⟞⟡⟞

The breakneck ride down the hill and into the tunnel of trees that spanned the road had been one long whoop for Con. As he entered the trees, the leaves and branches smeared into a blur of speed at the corners of his eyes. *Watch me now!* he thought. All at once, there was a rider beside him. *Haystacks perhaps, but why's he's riding so close?* Con raised an arm to push him away, but immediately a hand closed over it and he found himself being lifted from his saddle.

As the other three children reined in, men rose out of the vegetation on each side like highway robbers. They knew their jobs, grabbing the ponies' reins and dragging their riders sideways from their saddles. Sinéad found herself held by the scruff of the neck. Ahead of her, Con was putting up a brave fight.

'Watch that little one – he's like a fighting cock!' someone yelled.

'Le' go of me!' Con shouted. 'How dare you! That's my ship out there, my father's expecting me! Hands off!' The only serious fights Con had ever been in were dog-fights, and dogs know how to defend themselves.

'Damn it! He bit me!' cursed the man who was engulfing him.

'Don't bite him, son, you might poison yourself,' laughed a tall, bearded man – their leader, it appeared. 'Well, whose son are you, then? Son of the captain, eh?'

'Yes! And ... and ... he'll have you for p...piracy!'

The man let out a roar of laughter. '*Parlez vous français?* My cock sparrow, you're no sailor's son! Look at the flag, she's a French boat. I've known O'Neills of all shapes and sizes, and you just happen to be a small one. You'll have to whistle for that boat, son. I need to have something to hand over to the English when they hear I've let your Daddy sail away from here with his head on his shoulders. You'll do very nicely.'

Whistle for the boat ... Whistle for the boat, why not? thought Sinéad. All attention was now focused on Con, whose hands were held fast. *At least I can warn Haystacks!* She put her fingers in her mouth, took a breath, and blew a blast that raised a cloud of cawing rooks from the trees above.

The man with the beard whipped around, glared at her and snapped, 'Kill that boy!', and that was how it felt, a buffet on the side of her head that set her ears singing. A huge palm was slapped over her mouth, while rough fingers quickly bound her hands behind her back. There was no more banter. They even gagged her with someone's sweaty head-band; being a boy wasn't always fun. She was tied in a line with the others then, and marched off in the direction of the village ahead, carefully screened from the anchored boat by their captors. The bearded leader stalked beside

them; he had long greying hair, but walked like a young man. At
first he seemed unarmed, but then she noticed a squire marching a
pace behind him carrying his shield and a six-foot battleaxe. *A Gallowglass warrior!* she thought with awe.

Hugh O'Neill's head shot up from where he had been leaning over
the rail of the boat. 'A whistle! Catherine, did you hear that? Con's
whistle, I'd swear!' His hands gripped the transom rail. He turned,
but his wife had gone below. *'Monsieur le Capitaine,'* he shouted,
'call the Countess!' When the captain looked blank, he mimed the
Countess's prominent bulge, and the man understood immediately. Catherine came laboriously up the steep steps a few
moments later; she was very pregnant.

'You've seen him?' she asked eagerly.

'No, but I heard his whistle. Listen ...' They strained together.

'Con, my son, my precious one – are you there?' she whispered.
She turned to Hugh, a frown on her still beautiful face. 'The
MacSweeneys would never take him, would they?'

'Shhh ...' they leaned on the rail again, willing together for
another whistle. 'MacSweeney attacked our men, you know, when
we tried to take on fresh water.'

'Didn't we take one of their cows?'

'Not so as you'd notice – the cow belonged to an Englishman,
anyway.' Then he flared, 'Damn them!' and smashed his hand on
the rail. 'The MacSweeneys fostered Red Hugh, and we fought

side by side, one of them even saved my life, now they won't let us even re-victual our ship! Look at them there, marching up and down. We have sixteen cannon on this ship. If only we had room below to fire the damned things, I'd blast them off their Donegal rock!' He softened, and touched his wife's hand. 'Go below, my love. We have John and Brian on board, and whatever small life you carry inside you. Go, look after your young.' He turned back to his watching. The light began to fade.

Oh Con, oh Con, thought Hugh O'Neill, *you're the very fibre of my heart, my own rascal horse-boy. God knows what the English will do to you if they ever get you. Feed you on cream, as they did me, before taking all our lands, or lock you up as they did young Red Hugh? They'll use you as a stick to beat me, one way or another. So just keep your head – literally, I mean – and stay out of the Tower of London, son, it's so damp, so dangerous.*

The captain came up beside him and fidgeted.

Hugh pre-empted him. 'No, Captain, we must wait a little longer. He's out there. I can feel him. Till midnight, I beg of you.'

The building they were taken to had been severely damaged; it looked now like a cross between a barracks and a church. Their captors called it 'The Priory', which explained its mullioned windows and pointed arches. Once out of sight of the ship, they were lined up for inspection, and were surprised when the leader of the band turned with a tight little smile and said: 'Welcome to Fanad.

I am Domhnall MacSweeney – The MacSweeney, head of the clan – and I suspect you of illegal activity relating to the ship moored off my shore. Who are you and what are you doing in Rathmullan?'

They nudged Fion forward. 'Sir, there is nothing illegal in our activity – and despite your rude welcome, I am happy give you our names.' Fion then went on to explain how they had crossed Ireland to find Con, and had brought him here to Rathmullan to join his father who was, at this very moment, waiting for him on the boat moored in the bay outside. 'Sir,' he concluded, 'my uncle remembers with gratitude your past support and friendship. I am sure he is expecting you to let us deliver Con into his care. After this we will leave and will cause you no further trouble.'

'Very pretty,' said The MacSweeney. 'But it is *I*, boy, who will judge on the value of past friendships. Hugh O'Neill has enough sons on board to hand him his cup. To me, however, you have a certain value. We hold this building – what's left of it – for the English, and I wish to keep it. We built it as a priory a hundred years ago as a place of sanctuary.' His face twisted into a bitter smile. 'Then King Henry threw out our friars, and George Bingham wrecked it. All week I have turned a blind eye to the stream of nobles paddling out to that boat like a line of ducks. I think some small change is due to me. I too have to keep the bloody English off my back!' He was almost shouting now. 'The only thing the Prior ever needed to keep under lock and key was his wine. His wine cellar will keep you very nicely. Take them away!'

'What did he mean, small change?' asked Sinéad.

'He means he will hand us all over to the English as a sop for let-ting the boat sail,' said Fion.

'He's a bitter man,' declared Sinéad.

It must have been midnight when they heard a clatter on the dun-geon stairs. The door opened and the four occupants blinked in the light as men burst in carrying torches.

'Bring the young lad,' a voice called. One of them moved towards Sinéad. 'No, no, not the dark one, the redhead. Put a gag in his mouth, we don't want another whistle.'

Con didn't fight against them even when he was manhandled up from the cellar with a lot less respect than the Prior's wines. When he was marched through the great hall, heads turned as he passed, as people turn to watch a condemned man being taken to the gallows. Con sensed that something momentous was happen-ing. He straightened his shoulders. There was a low murmur of approval, sympathy even. When they came to the winding stairs, he snapped.

'Leave me, I won't run away,' so they let him walk freely until he emerged onto the leaded walkway behind improvised battlements on the priory roof.

At first Con could see little, but when they quenched the torches the whole sweep of the estuary appeared, and on it floated a ghostlike ship, silvery in the starlight. Its sails were full now, slanting across the wind, its wake was like a snail's trail on the dark water. A light moved on the quarter-deck – *Father!*

Hugh O'Neill leaned on the rail behind the helmsman, staring back down the ship's wake ... staring at all he was leaving behind: an island, a nation, a dream, and one small son.

CHAPTER 19

Kiss the Hag

On a height above the town, a shadowy figure stood watching the vanishing ship. He had seen the small figure on the priory walls. *So they have him still.* He looked up at the canopy of stars and noted the halo about the moon. Bad weather coming, but he had a duty to perform. He must compose, if only in his mind, a lament for the departure of Hugh O'Neill, Earl of Tyrone, and the noble shipload of chiefs who were going with him.

This would have to be a lament on a grand scale and in the ancient form, in which men are taller than trees, and women fairer than ever they were in life; where mountains rise up to the sky, and cattle and pigs multiply until you could walk across Ireland on their backs. Even as the phrases rolled over in his mind, he knew that they belonged to an older age. This was the end of his Ireland, the end of his culture, the Gaelic culture. O'Neill would never return, and poets like himself would fade and be gone.

A constriction began in his throat, but then, unbidden, a sudden thought crossed his mind: *Perhaps there is something I can save out of this.* He looked down at the priory. *Four new seeds to plant if I can get them out of there. I even have an apprentice!* He smiled. *Perhaps we won't fade, after all, perhaps we will just change.* The lights had all gone out in the tower below. *Now, how on earth can I get them out?*

<hr />

In the pitch dark of the Prior's wine cellar they waited anxiously for Con's return.

'It's not dawn yet, is it?' Sinéad asked.

'No, more like midnight,' answered Séamus. 'Why?'

'It's just that they take prisoners to be executed at dawn. They wouldn't hurt Con, surely? That MacSweeney – he's so cold!' Sinéad shivered.

Half an hour passed, then there were sounds of steps on the stairs again. The door opened, throwing a mat of yellow light onto the broken flags of the dungeon floor and Con's small form stumbled on to it. With a mocking, 'Sleep well, son', the guard closed the door and Con was left to shuffle cautiously to his place on the cold, stone shelf that once held barrels and now served the children as a bed. Sinéad slid along the shelf towards him.

'Well?' one of the boys asked from the darkness.

'He's gone,' was all Con could whisper.

Sinéad reached out and found, first an arm, and then his hand.

He resisted, but after a moment he slid towards her; he rested his head against her shoulder for a moment, and sniffed. 'You smell of Aoife.' She smiled; it wasn't exactly a compliment, but if it comforted him ... She imagined the two of them, from four years old, curled up together like pups in that big family bed. She put an arm around him and pulled him towards her.

The guard who opened the door in the morning jabbed a torch into the bracket on the wall and glared at them.

'Looks as if the chief intends to keep you alive for a bit, after all,' he said, putting down a basket. 'Fresh bread and hard-boiled eggs,' he announced, 'better'n I get!' He scratched his head. 'Now, what was I to tell you? Oh yes. There will be a clan gathering tonight. The usual humble fare: roasted ox that's been hanging for a week – ripe as a peach it is – a fat pig, and a couple of last year's lambs. Followed by the usual blather, music and song, a fight or two, perhaps – and if we get really bored, a hanging! The chief'll decide on your fate then.' He eyed the children. 'Eat up, scrub up, and shut up, that's my advice. That way you'll be clean for the feast – or the hanging!' He chuckled. 'There's water'n soap in the corner, and a bucket for soil. If you want anything more, ask Calum. That's him whistling – he'd drive a saint to drink.'

The whistling was getting closer and there was the sound of steps on the stairs. They expected a young man, but Calum looked to be about the same age as the chief. He was carrying their packs which he now dropped on the floor at the door. They had obviously been gone through, but otherwise looked intact.

'Don't mind Ronan,' he said, 'he was just trying to cheer you up – in his own way. I'll be looking after you.' He reached up and unlatched some shutters high in their prison wall; weak morning light filtered down through an iron grille. 'Don't forget your breakfast.' Then he went out, bolted the door, and his whistling receded.

'The Ronan one – he didn't mean it about the hanging, did he?' wondered Sinéad.

'I think that was his idea of a joke,' said Fion. 'But the bread smells good. Perhaps the chief will be in a better mood now that the boat's gone. A lot of these MacSweeneys are still Gallowglasses at heart – you'd have to be half-mad to swear to die before you surrender, like Gallowglasses do, and you'd have to be equally mad to get on the wrong side of them. We'll just have to lie low–'

There was a sudden eruption from the bench where Séamus had been sitting. 'Lie low? Aren't we even going to try to escape? Where's my pack? Look in your packs, everyone,' he commanded as he tore his open. 'Have they left us any weapons? I'm not going to rot here, Gallowglasses or not.' They caught his mood and searched thoroughly, but there wasn't as much as a penknife between them. Séamus threw his pack down in disgust. 'Here, Fion, give me a leg-up. Let's look at the grille up there; it looks rusted through to me.' Fion cupped his hands for Séamus's foot, and heaved as he sprang. For a moment Séamus hung, swinging from the grille, and sending down a shower of rust, but it didn't move an inch. He dropped back to the ground and bent forward to brush the rust out of his hair. 'Those bars must be an inch thick,' he said in disgust. 'Damn it, how did we get ourselves into this pickle?'

'It was my fault, riding ahead.' Con's voice sounded small.

Sinéad turned on him. 'No, Con, it was not your fault! We all rode down that hill like mad things. We're all to blame. The only one who showed any sense was Haystacks. I wonder if he got away? Surely if they'd caught him they'd have brought him down here. You're right, Séamus, we mustn't give up, and the best thing is for us to be prepared. What did grouchy Ronan say? "Eat up, scrub up, and shut up?" I'm going to scrub up first. You gentlemen can start breakfast – but leave me my share.'

They washed in turns, and Sinéad blessed her boy's-length hair – at least she could comb it. Hearing Calum whistling outside, they called for more water, and got it. He had just put down the bucket when he caught sight of Sinéad and blinked: 'Hey laddie, where'd you get that pretty face?' With a shock she realised she'd parted her wet fringe like a girl. She blew him a raspberry and hastily tousled her hair again.

They had no knives, so all the food had to be broken up by hand. As Sinéad cracked an egg, she remembered the last cooked meal she'd had, that memorable stew in the herdsmen's camp, with Aoife watching every spoonful. 'I wish I could have a bowlful of that stew Aoife gave me at the O'Brolchains,' she said wistfully.

Con looked up, an anxious look on his face: 'You didn't eat it, did you?' Then he shook his head. 'You know, Sinéad, that stew was the self-same stew I was given the day I arrived with them three years ago. You see, each day, we throw in whatever comes to hand – a fist-full of oats, a hat-full of barley, bits of cow, chunks of deer, gobbets of sheep, wild boar, hedgehogs – prickles off, if we have time – badgers, squirrels ... let me think: snails, frogs ...'

'Ah go on with you!' laughed Sinéad. 'Why don't you tell the others about the crab-apples and the English scouts?'

As the day wore on they ran out of stories to tell and listened instead to the wind rising outside.

'How do you get to Spain?' Con asked, glancing anxiously up at the tossing branches they could see through the grille.

'They will sail down the length of Ireland and then south across the Bay of Biscay,' Fion replied. They looked at each other; they all knew about the Bay of Biscay, birthplace of storms, and wondered about Uncle Hugh's boat, battling with wind and wave.

As the light outside faded, the roar of the clan gathering upstairs grew until eventually it drowned out the sound of the wind. Calum and Ronan came in, carrying a length of chain.

'Stand close together and put one foot forward,' Ronan ordered. The two then clamped ankle-rings around the children's legs, and linked these onto the chain. 'This little fella here could nearly step out of his ring!' Calum observed. 'Don't disgrace me by running away, son, will you?' Con told him it would be a pleasure, and blinked at the smell of strong drink off him. 'Carry the chain between you as you walk,' the man ordered.

Off they went in a line up the steep flight of stairs from their dungeon, through a pointed church-like arch, and into a hall already thronged with men. To their left was a high table, with a canopied chair for the chief. They were to sit at a side table looking diagonally across at the chief's chair. They had to shuffle in, in front of their bench, on account of their chains. The air was full of the smell of damp clothing, smoking torches, and the more welcome smell of food, much of which was already set out on the tables where the feasters would soon help themselves. Only the high table had servers. Two tall, longhaired Gallowglass warriors in padded jerkins and bright mail stood on each side of the chief's chair, their fearsome battleaxes flashing as they moved. The seated men had beakers of mead to hand, the few ladies held glasses of wine.

There was a stir as Domhnall MacSweeney strode in. Everyone rose, including the children. He placed his lady to his right, and then stood in front of his carved chair. He cut a fine figure with his spade-like beard washed and combed. Both he and his wife were richly dressed in embroidered silks, and she flashed with jewels. As they took their places, a young man with a glowering expression and a newly bandaged head sat down on their left.

Calum, who was standing behind the children, bent to whisper in Fion's ear, 'That's Domhnall Óg, his son. Now there'll be the toast; you'd best drink too.'

'The MacSweeney!' roared the two Gallowglass warriors. The children reached for the ale that had been provided for them and drank.

Then Domhnall MacSweeney turned towards them with a tight smile. 'Ladies and gentlemen, a toast to our young guests, who had the misfortune to miss their boat last night!' There was a ripple of laughter as all eyes turned on the children, some hostile, more just curious; they drank.

'I'd watch that smile,' whispered Calum, who seemed to have taken on the job of keeping Fion informed. 'Domhnall's got something on his mind. There's trouble brewing.'

Sure enough, the chief had another toast to make: 'To my son, Domhnall Óg, for his valiant attack on the Earl of Tyrone's watering party.'

Fion looked closely at the young man with the bandaged head, who was now scowling at the gathering. There were uncertain grins, but everyone drank. Fion leaned back and whispered to Calum: 'What's going on? Mocking his own son?'

Calum grinned. 'Domhnall Óg happened on a party from that French boat yesterday; they were filling barrels with fresh water for their voyage. There'd been some talk about the French stealing a cow, so he decided to attack them, but he botched it and only just got away with his life. Domhnall senior is *not* pleased; imagine a son of The MacSweeney routed by a watering party?'

'Do you know the chief well?'

'Been with him since I was a pup, my mother was his wet nurse.

Though a free man, I'm a common kern, but the chief and I are almost blood. I know him and he knows me. He knew the Earl was sailing – he's not blind – all these grand folk rowing across at dead of night. We could have stopped them, just as we stopped you, but old loyalties are still strong. Red Hugh O'Donnell, your Uncle O'Neill's closest ally, was our chief's foster brother. You see how it goes. When he learned that Red Hugh's brother, Donal, was on board he decided not to betray them. So the boat's gone, but the English will demand a price.'

'Us?' queried Fion.

Calum nodded.

'What will the chief do with us?'

'Give you over to the English, at a guess. The little redhead lad,' he tipped his head towards Con, 'the Earl's son – he'll be worth a purse or two of gold and perhaps a knighthood for the chief, one day! It's a shame, though, to put a young lad in the Tower of London. They'll be along quick enough when they hear about the ship, so having you and the young lad to hand over will take the sting out of it. I reckon, though, he wants the clan's support for handing you over before we all get too drunk to think. I better do some serving.' Calum got up stiffly from where he'd been squatting.

Sinéad, who had been listening, glanced at Fion beside her. 'They won't split us up, will they?' she asked. 'You'd be worth a purse of gold too, you know.'

Fion gave an unconvinced shrug. 'I think not; who'd want me?'

'Well, I would!' she said, so strongly that she blushed. *We all belong together. Is there no one to help us?* Her eyes swept the room, and then stopped. There, among all those faces, was one she recognised. *Yes!* She gripped Fion's arm. 'Don't look now,' she whispered, 'but we have a poet in our midst! It's Haystacks, and he's free – but what can he do?' Her eyes moved to Domhnall. The chief was glancing at his bodyguards; the business was about to begin. *Come on, Haystacks! Whatever it is – do it now!*

<hr />

The warriors stepped forward, one on each side of their chief, and roared for silence. Domhnall MacSweeney rose to his feet and quenched any remaining conversation with a look.

'Gentlemen, before we break bread and while our heads are clear, we have a small matter to decide – or, to be accurate, four small matters.' Heads turned to the children. 'Let me present to you Con O'Neill, son of Hugh O'Neill, the Earl of Tyrone.' People moved, craning to look. 'Con, pray stand.' Con stood, sparking defiance, ready at any second to give this MacSweeney a piece of his mind. Sinéad kicked him, and their shackles clanked. Con tossed his head. 'Next we have Fion O'Neill, a nephew of Hugh O'Neill.' Fion rose and bowed. 'And finally we have Séamus and Brian de Cashel, Norman followers of the Earl.' They both stood. 'Yesterday, for reasons beyond their control–'

'Beyond our–!' Con's indignant squeak was again cut short by Sinéad, this time by a dig in the ribs.

The chief managed a tight smile. 'As I say, for reasons beyond their control, they were unable to join the ship that sailed yester-day. We would naturally like to offer our young guests hospitality here, but it is my opinion that in view of their high birth it would be more proper for them to be guests of King James.'

Calum's right – he's handing us over to the English! thought Sinéad.

'However, gentlemen,' The MacSweeney continued, 'I need your wise counsel and approval before I proceed. Pray, speak up.'

The silence stretched and stretched. No one was going to go against the chief. Also, they were hungry.

Where are you, Haystacks? It's now or never. Do something, please, and quick! Sinéad was getting very anxious. The men were losing interest, their mouths were watering, they wanted to eat. *Domhnall's chosen this moment on purpose!* Now he was bending forward as if to pick up the heavy mace that lay on the table in front of him, presumably to mark the end of clan business. At long last, a loud, clear voice rang out from the bottom of the hall, and Sinéad nearly collapsed with relief.

'My Lord! I crave permission to address you and your noble clan.'

Heads whipped around in protest; surely not now, while meat was on the table! But Sinéad's glance was for the chief, who looked perplexed.

'We know you not, sir,' MacSweeney replied, 'nor by what right you assume to speak at this gathering.'

'I have no right to speak here except the right granted to my profession as a poet. I have, however, something to say on the past greatness of your clan.'

'Well, can't it wait until we have our business done and have eaten our fill?'

'No, sir, because what you propose to do with these young people does not sit easily with the greatness of which I speak. I merely ask that your decision be postponed until I have had my say.'

'According to tradition, I must welcome you as a poet, but I dare not keep these people from their meat. We will postpone our decision, but you too will have to wait until our hunger is satisfied.' At this the chief turned to his wife and began talking to her loudly about his dogs; the noise in the room rose as everyone's attention turned to the food in front of them.

For a while Sinéad couldn't even think of eating, but then, seeing Haystacks tucking in, she too set to. He had won the first round – no decision had been made.

Eventually the flow of conversation eased, men pushed the debris of their meal away, or threw it to the dogs. Legs stretched comfortably under the tables and faces turned in anticipation to this unknown poet, who was now thanking them for their hospitality. Sinéad watched, fascinated, as Haystacks gradually wooed their attention before launching into a tale as old as the clan itself.

'Hear you, men, young and old, descendants of Niall – Niall of the Nine Hostages – open your ears because while swords make history, it is the poet's word that makes history live.'

They must have heard this story a hundred times, because the MacSweeneys claimed descent from the mythical Niall, but it was as if everyone in the room was hearing it for the first time. Young Niall, returning as a man to his father's court, where his step-mother and her four favoured sons ruled the roost, lived again in the listener's minds. Which of the king's sons would succeed his father when he died? Niall was favoured by the people, but his stepmother naturally favoured her sons, and so she engaged Sith-chenn, a clever druid, to test them. Sithchenn gave the five boys a task: to save just one object from a burning forge. Sinéad could almost feel the heat and smoke of the fire when Haystacks described how Niall struggled out carrying the anvil, judged the most sensible thing to have saved from the forge.

Next, Sithchenn sent Niall and his half-brothers out to hunt. All day they ran through the forest without drink or rest, until their tongues swelled in their mouths and their legs would hardly carry them. One after the other, they came to a clearing in the forest where a spring of the purest water bubbled out of the ground, but as each approached the spring he found himself con-fronted by a hag so ugly, so repulsive that his stomach turned. 'One kiss, my boy, just one kiss, and you can drink your fill,' the hag cackled. One after another the boys approached, only to turn away, retching in disgust. Lastly Niall stepped forward and their lips touched (Sinéad's face wrinkled in distaste); he kissed and did not flinch, and at that moment he found in his arms the fairest maid in all Ireland.

There was a sigh of satisfaction from the whole company. Sinéad sighed too, opened her eyes, and found herself looking directly into the eyes of Domhnall MacSweeney. The mocking smile was gone – could it mean indecision? But the moment passed, the eyes clouded over, and the tight smile returned. Now came a crash at the far end of the hall. The door was thrown back and a man, glistening from the storm outside, staggered in, thrusting the drunken revellers aside.

'My Lord!' he cried. 'The English are on the road!'

There was pandemonium in the hall. Sinéad watched as Domhnall MacSweeney rose to his feet. *He's got us now, hasn't he, all neatly chained, ready to trade,* she thought bitterly. The intensity of his gaze almost burned, but now Haystacks was on the move, thrusting men aside until he and The MacSweeney stood face to face across the high table. Sinéad saw their eyes meet and lock. The guards stirred uneasily, but Haystacks fought with words, not steel. Just three words, delivered like dagger thrusts: one, two, three.

Domhnall MacSweeney visibly winced as the words struck home. Sinéad half-expected him to fall stricken, but no, on the contrary he seemed to grow taller, gathering strength as he grew, suddenly magnificent.

He turned towards the children, pointed at them and roared: 'Calum! Get the chains off those children and get them the hell out of here!'

And he turned to Con with a curt nod: chief to son-of-chief. Con returned this with dignity.

'Does that mean you're to slit our throats?' Fion asked as Calum plunged about at his feet undoing their shackles.

'Not this time, sir.' The man was grinning from ear to ear. 'He's done what's right, and he knows it. Him and me, we didn't share life's breakfast for nothing.' Even the grouch Ronan grinned as he grumbled, struggling with Calum to undo their chains.

Despite her delight, Sinéad suddenly felt uneasy, She felt eyes on her, predatory eyes! *Who could have an interest in us now?* she wondered. Then she saw him, staring at them with a fierce intensity – Domhnall Óg MacSweeney.

It took them barely ten minutes to pack their saddlebags and be ready for the road again. 'Where's Haystacks?' Fion asked as they pushed their way up the stairs and out through the still crowded hall. Hefty pats on the back helped them on and out into the courtyard. There, in the flickering light, stood Haystacks, anonymous again in his shaggy mantle, holding his horse and a fistful of reins. Sinéad wanted to run up and hug him, but remembered just in time that she was still Brian.

They heard Calum whistling and then he came mounted on a jennet to go with them. 'All I could get,' he said.

Once again they were on their way, facing north-west, the English behind them, and a fresh gale in their faces.

Between the Devil and the sea, thought Sinéad.

CHAPTER 20

The Final Pursuit

alum had to return to the priory, but they would be safe for a while in the fisherman's hut he had found for them. As he opened the door to leave, the sound of wind and wave rose to a crescendo; both he and his whistling seemed to be snatched away by the wind. A single wick, floating in a saucer of seal oil, was their only light; it fluttered and then recovered. For the first time since their mad dash into MacSweeney's ambush, they were free and alone together, this time lounging on piles of fisherman's nets, dry because the storm had put paid to all fishing.

Séamus propped himself on an elbow and turned to Haystacks. 'How did you do it?' he asked. 'I am still convinced MacSweeney was going to hand us over to the English. What did you say to him?'

'It can't have been more than four words,' said Fion. 'I was watching.'

'No, three!' said Sinéad triumphantly. 'Don't tell them,

Haystacks. I want to guess.' She kept them waiting, then said: 'KISS ... THE ... HAG! Am I right?'

Haystacks laughed. 'Well done, Sinéad!'

There were murmurs of appreciation until Con complained: 'Will somebody please tell me what's going on?'

They all started to explain until Sinéad cut in: 'It's like this, Con. In his heart of hearts MacSweeney wanted to let us go – he's an Irish chieftain, after all, and it's a matter of honour – but the temptation to sell us to the English was too strong. The temptation was his "horrible hag" like in the Niall story, that turned into the fairest maid. And when Haystacks told him to "kiss the hag" he was saying, "Do what you know is right" – like what you did when you sent Aoife your gold pebble.'

Con thought for a moment, then a mischievous grin crossed his face. 'Poor Aoife – some fair maid!' For the first time in a long while, they all laughed together.

An hour later Calum came in, soaked to the knees having walked through the tide so his footprints wouldn't lead straight to the hut. 'Well, I've got news for you,' he announced.

'Have they arrested MacSweeney?' Haystacks asked.

Calum shook his head. 'No, he's stuffing them with food and drink, but listen to this. The reason they're here is that they heard yesterday of a French ship sheltering here in Lough Swilly.'

'Of course. That'll be the Earl's boat,' said Haystacks.

'No, not the Earl's boat. This one is smaller. She was seen from Inishowen opposite – she's probably a French wine boat returning from Derry with wool or butter.'

'A second boat!' exclaimed Haystacks, heaving himself to his feet. 'Where is she now?'

'She's up at Portsalon, the first sheltered cove in the bay.' Their hut shook in the wind. 'And she won't be sailing tonight, I can tell you.'

'Look, Calum,' said Haystacks urgently, 'I *must* check out this boat immediately!' He dropped his voice. 'I don't care where she's going, but we've got to get young Con out of here. How long before someone spills the beans and tells the English that Con was left behind?'

'Hard to say. They and their horses are exhausted, and Domhnall is giving them enough drink to drown them. They know that the Earl sailed yesterday and will presume Con's on board. Just one man worries me – an Englishman who speaks funny. He's been asking after a group of children, but says one of them's a girl ...' Sinéad looked away quickly as Calum glanced around. *Bonmann!* she thought, old fears churning in her stomach.

But now Haystacks was on his feet. 'That clinches it. I must be off again and find out what I can about this mysterious boat. Calum, will you guide me?' Calum nodded. 'Rest as much as you can, and let's hope she won't sail before we get to her. If you need to go out, be careful, and don't leave tracks in the sand.'

'How I wish I could sail with you, Con!' exclaimed Séamus, slashing at the air with an imagined sword. 'I bet there's an Irish regiment I could join. Don't you realise, Sinéad, we've got nothing to go back to. Can you imagine being bottled up in Dundalk with Aunt Fee?'

'Perhaps I should accept the beastly piglet's proposal?' she said bitterly.

'I think Bonmann's interest is murder now rather than marriage. You see, we can't lay claim to our heritage from the grave,' said Séamus. 'Anyway, I want a new start. I will fight for Ireland from Spain.'

'It's a French boat, so it's probably going to France,' said Sinéad acidly.

'Who cares, there are Irish regiments there too. I wish I'd paid more attention to Fenton's French lessons.'

'You were too busy learning Latin!' said Sinéad through her teeth, then regretted it. 'I don't want to leave Ireland ever. What about you, Fion?'

'I'd stay if I had a future here. I should join up with Uncle Hugh, but what use would I be? Then there is so much to be learned – about the stars, new lands, new people. What I'd really like is a good education. The priesthood is cheap, they say, but I don't think it would suit me – I'm more interested in this earth than in heaven, really. Anyway, we haven't the money for a night's lodging, let alone a passage to France. A sea captain might take an Earl's son in the hope of being paid later, but not a load of raga-muffins like us.'

'I'll become a nun, and pray for your souls – and for the souls of other lost causes.'

It was the following evening before Haystacks returned. By now they were all as cross as cats, and never wanted to see another fish-net in their lives. When he arrived, he stood inside the door, sway-ing from exhaustion.

'No questions now, I'm dropping. But I have news for you. Thanks to Calum, I have spoken to the captain of the *St Lucia*. She is indeed French, and is returning from Derry with wool and hides. He has no cabin for passengers, but the wool sacks would make comfortable enough beds. At any rate, he's agreed to take four passengers provided they are on the beach at Portsalon by tomorrow evening. He reckons the storm will have blown itself out by then. We will set out at dawn. Start thinking now about whether or not you wish to go. Con, you must go for your own safety, and one of the others should go with you. Fion, you might be the best one to accompany Con. As for you, Séamus and Sinéad, there is room for you to go too, if you wish.'

'But sir, we have no money,' said Séamus.

'Decide what you would really like to do, and we'll talk ways and means tomorrow. Sleep on it. That's what I'm going to do.'

With that, he threw himself down on the nets, covered himself with his mantle, and was soon snoring gently.

❧

Overnight the wind dropped and they woke to drips and the sound of drumming rain on thin thatch. When they opened the door they found themselves looking out through a vertical screen of rain that seemed to have hammered the waves into a reluctant calm.

'This will be the end of the storm,' said Haystacks. 'Hopefully it's blown itself out. We will go as soon as the rain eases. Close the door. I have a weight on my mind – or rather, around my neck.' Haystacks lifted the strap of a small but heavy satchel over his head. He turned to Con. 'Your father, Con, gave me money to use as I thought best, first to find you, and then to bring you to Rathmullan in time for his sailing. Well, I failed in that, but there is enough money here to pay for your passage and to see you well on your way to finding your father in Spain. But this isn't all yours, Con.' He smiled and turned to Séamus. 'Your father also gave me a sum in gold for the three of you – yes, Fion, you too are to have your share. His hope was to have you all safe out of Ireland while he secured the castle in Séamus's name. Whether or not you go now, I will give you all your shares. Take the money and hide it, not in your packs, but on your bodies somewhere. I have given the French captain enough money to keep him at anchor until you come on board; later I'll tell you how much to pay him when your journey's safely over.'

They had hardly finished hiding their gold in pouches and belts – Sinéad even sewed coins into the seam of her cloak – when they heard the sound of galloping hooves coming straight to the door.

Calum burst in. 'Come quickly – quickly – we must fly! You remember the man who speaks funny? Well, he has a friend – fat, looks like a priest–'

'Fenton!' Séamus snarled.

'So, Bonmann didn't hang him, then!' said Haystacks. 'There's a devil's partnership, but go on.'

'Denounces you as fugitives and reckons you will be making for the new boat at Portsalon – everyone knows about it now – but Domhnall's men are refusing to help him. This gives us a chance. Without a guide, they'll have to follow the road. But I know a short cut through the mountains that will save us an hour or more. We must be off the road and out of sight before they catch up, so hurry.'

They were practised now, and were saddled-up and on the road in less than ten minutes. They cantered in line, keeping to the crown of the road to hide their tracks until Calum led them off the road and into a well-concealed boreen.

They'd never have found the path without Calum to guide them as it wound in and out between huge boulders and crags, hugging a shoulder-high cliff between the mountains and the sea. Séamus was riding eagerly on Calum's heels. The scenery was wild and beautiful. Haystacks dropped back to keep Sinéad company.

'And you, Sinéad? Will you go?'

She didn't answer for a while, gazing about her at the heather slopes, the yellow lichened rocks, and the sea which was turning from grey to green to blue. *How could I ever want to leave here?* she thought.

'You know, Haystacks,' she said after a little while, 'what I would really, really like would be for you to say to me: Sinéad – or perhaps Brian – I need an apprentice. Come with me and I will teach you the poems of Amergin, and the Tain, and how to play the harp ...' She looked over at him, anxious that he might be laughing at her, but he wasn't.

'You know, Sinéad,' he said, 'there is nothing in the world that I would like better. I can see us now: the poet and his boy. I've never had an apprentice or even a companion on the road.'

'I would gather nuts for us, I could cook,' said Sinéad, warming to the theme, 'and you would tell me the meaning of things like who really is "the wind that breathes upon the sea".'

They rode on, happily planning their wandering life, until the moment when they topped the rise, and the bay of Portsalon spread out below them. Sinéad could only gasp. To their left was an arc of the whitest sand she had ever seen, creaming waves curving in towards it, and out there in the clear blue water, like a child's model, floated a neat little ship, with the flag of France flying at her mast.

For the first time since they had left the road, they looked back – and got the shock of their lives.

There they were, a line of horsemen, threading their way up the slope scarcely a mile behind them. All hope of a leisurely departure vanished. At the head of the line rode a man in a white hat.

'Domhnall Óg!' Calum swore. 'That's his bandage. He's acting as their guide. Damn him for a traitor.'

They looked at the rocky path ahead – no headlong rush down there! But Calum was busy. He pulled a pistol from his belt and poured a generous measure of black powder down the barrel, followed this by a wad, then a ball, and rammed them home.

'We can't hold them off with that!' said Haystacks.

'No, but perhaps I can alert the captain of the ship. It's going to be touch and go; it'll take time to launch their boat and row for the shore. Stand back in case this thing explodes.' The bang was impressive, as was the spurt of smoke.

'Come on,' urged Calum. 'Domhnall Óg will have heard that too. We've to get down off the mountain, and it's a good mile along the beach to where they can land.'

The ponies were nimble on the mountain, slipping and sliding down on their haunches. As the children waited for Calum and Haystacks at the bottom, they looked up. Their pursuers were having trouble; two of them appeared to have fallen and were leading their horses. Only one was travelling fast, his white head bobbing as he expertly zigzagged down the path after them.

'Look, they've launched a boat,' cheered Con.

'They'll land at the mouth of the river,' shouted Haystacks. 'Follow Calum, he'll show you where the sand is hardest.'

With heads down into the wind, they set out after Calum, galloping through the chasing waves. Spray flew and seagulls screeched. From time to time they would glimpse the rowing boat as it rose on a wave, its oars flashing. Was it making progress? Sinéad looked back once and saw that Domhnall Óg had reached the sand; she urged her pony on. They reached the river before the boat and Calum led them into the sandhills where they were out of the wind and out of sight of their pursuers. Here it became a frenzy of activity.

Haystacks was issuing orders. 'The boat's too small to take four, so you will have to go in pairs. Con, you and Séamus go first, then Fion and Sinéad. You will have to carry your packs, so get them ready now.'

Sinéad, designated to the second boat, had time to climb to where Calum was watching from the lip of the dune. The boat was still a hundred yards or more from the shore.

'It will be close,' said Calum. 'Look how fast Domhnall's coming!'

Why Domhnall? Sinéad wondered. *What does he want with us? Who does he want?* Then she had it: *Con! It has to be Con. He will snatch him while he runs. For a reward, yes, but for pride too. One in the eye for O'Neill for the watering party incident.* Instantly, she knew what she had to do. Without wasting a second, she surfed down the dune and launched herself at Con.

'Con, your shirt. Give me your shirt! No, don't argue!' she yelled as she dragged his precious yellow shirt up and over his head, thrusting her plain garment at him; they were one of a size. 'Put that on.'

'Ready!' shouted Calum. As a last measure she pulled Con's hat down over his red hair. 'Go – GO – run for the boat!' As Con and Séamus ran, she scrambled up the dune to watch.

Calum had his pistol in his hand. There were the boys pelting across the sand – but where was the boat? There! It seemed to rise out of the ocean, cresting the final wave, the men heaving on their oars.

And there came Domhnall Óg riding into the picture, aiming straight at the boys. Sinéad leapt to her feet and screamed. 'Run, Séamus, run!'

'Get down, get down!' said Calum, pulling at her.

But Domhnall had seen her – a flash of yellow on the dunes. She could almost hear his curse as he pulled on his reins and veered past the two fugitives towards her.

'My God!' said Calum. 'I thought you were Con for a moment.'

'Yes! So did Domhnall!' gasped Sinéad. 'It worked!'

⚜

She watched as Con and Séamus were hauled aboard and the boat broke out through the waves. Domhnall, turning his attention to the dunes, rode towards them, but a bullet in the sand from

Calum's pistol turned him away. Calum remained on watch as Domhnall cantered back to join the others. 'They'll leave us alone for a while, I think. They're exposed out there,' he said, reloading his pistol.

As it would be some time before the boat could return, Sinéad slid down the dune and walked back to where Haystacks was leading the ponies deeper into the dunes. She went up to her beloved pony, put her arm over her neck and buried her head in the pony's mane.

She glanced up and saw Haystacks looking at her expectantly. 'I want to stay,' she pleaded, 'but it's over, isn't it? Our dream: the poet and his boy?'

His smile was sad. 'Yes, and no, Sinéad. Yes, because you must go, and No because you will stay and ride forever in my heart. The others need you, and you need them. You see, you belong in the future, while I belong in the past. My world is fading now, and my role is to save what I can of it; yours is to sow the seeds of a new Ireland in whatever soil will nourish you.'

She said goodbye to her pony then, and to the other ponies for good measure, packed up her possessions and was ready to leave.

'What will happen to the ponies?' she asked Haystacks.

'I'll turn horse dealer for a while. Don't worry, I'll find the best of homes for them,' he reassured her.

'Ready?' called Calum from above.

She pulled her hat down firmly in case it fell off. But she couldn't move. The dunes – home – beckoned to her, but at that moment she felt Fion's hand in hers, and knew she would go.

'Come on!' he said, and off they went, racing across the sand. As before, Calum had timed their run to perfection; the boat was even now breaking through the final waves. She was vaguely aware of two horsemen galloping to intersect them. Fion increased their pace.

There was the boat ahead, swinging about to lie stern-on to shore. A sailor threw them a rope. Fion had let go of her hand to grab it. For a second she was left alone, the water swirling about her knees. She turned and screamed. Domhnall Óg was bearing down on her, spray spouting from his horse's hooves. *What does he want me for?* Then: *Holy smoke! It's not me – it's Con! He thinks I'm Con. I'm still wearing Con's shirt.*

It was too late to tear it off now. Domhnall was already leaning forward to grab her. In a second she'd be snatched up and thrown over his saddle. Instinctively, she tore her hat from her head and shook her hair free. She saw shock on his face: black hair, not red, then instant recognition – hadn't they stared at each other at the banquet? He had no use for her. With a wrench at his horse's reins he was past, hurling curses at her.

Fion was yelling for her to come, but she just stood, mesmerised. There in the air, at the sea's edge, waving his arms like some clumsy seabird, was her suitor, Sir Geoffrey Bonmann. His horse, head down and front legs braced, had at last rid itself of its hateful rider. Later, Sinéad would dine out on the story of Bonmann's plunge, but she would leave out his 'loving' words as he rose streaming with water: 'We'll get you all yet, you little bwats!'

Fion's grip on her arm was like a lifeline. In seconds they were being hauled over the stern of the boat. The cheering Frenchmen dug in their oars and the boat crashed out through the waves. Bundled in the stern, Fion held Sinéad as if to crush the life out of her.

'He won't get me, will he?' she gasped after a while.

'Over my dead body!' said Fion, holding her tighter still.

Haystacks chose a prominent place on the headland on which to stand. As the sails unfurled and the chanting of the sailors hauling the anchor carried across the water, he could see four small figures leaning over the stern rail. He waved, and they waved back. He thought of their hectic departure and smiled at the lingering image of Fion and Sinéad, hand in hand, running into the foam.

The boat would soon round the point. Now only one tiny figure remained standing at the rail, so the poet raised his arms again and sang for Sinéad the verses she had liked so much:

I am the wind which breathes upon the sea,

I am the wave of the ocean,

I am the murmur of the billows,

I am the ox of the seven combats,

I am the vulture upon the rocks,

I am the beam of the sun,

I am the fairest of plants ...

HISTORICAL NOTES ~ Fact and Fiction

These are the signatures of Hugh O'Neill, Earl of Tyrone,
from letters written by him in 1601.

ABOUT *FUGITIVES!*

'Until it was midnight and the stars were out Tyrone stood at the gunwale watching for Con,' wrote Seán O'Faolain in his wonderful book, *The Great O'Neill*. 'Who was Con?' I asked myself, 'and why was Hugh O'Neill waiting for him?'

That was where this story began. Most of the time history shows itself slowly, piece by piece, but then, occasionally, it can burst out and come alive, and we realise that these people were real, living, breathing and signing their names! Above are two copies of Hugh O'Neill's signatures. Think of him, as Sinéad saw him, quill in hand, writing a letter to King James King of England.

FACT OR FICTION?

Because Hugh O'Neill is one of the great men of Irish history, we know what he looked like and what sort of person he was. On the other hand, we know almost nothing about Con, so I had to imagine him. His father had red hair, so I give Con red hair. When Hugh O'Neill was taken to England as a boy he was dubbed 'that rascal horse-boy,' so I have imagined Con, like his father, getting up to mischief, and being a fine pony rider. The other children in the book, Fion, James/Séamus and Sinéad, are made up, but they live in a world of real castles, wars and intrigues. You can visit many of the places I describe (see the map in the front of the book) and, like me, try to imagine them as they once were.

NORMAN CASTLES

As Norman castles were built to similar designs, you will be able to recognise many of the features that were familiar to Sinéad and the others, in any castle you may visit. Near the door you should find the guard room – there may even be a murder hole through which one could shoot attackers at the door. The spiral stairs usually start about here and you can trace their climb from the slit windows. Inside you can count the floors from the holes where the beams were let into the walls. If you are allowed to climb to the roof, you can lean on the battlements like Uncle Hugh and Sinéad. You will, however, have to imagine the now vanished town of thatched houses and workshops that once clustered about the castle. Go to the rear of the castle and you may see where the garderobes (toilets) jutted out. If you had lived in the fifteenth century you would have got used to the strong castle smells.

Castle life was crowded; the windows were tiny, so it was quite dark inside. Light came from flaring torches, candles, and tiny rush lights. In summertime, people lived outside as much as possible. In times of danger, however, the family slept on the top floor where it was safest.

THE PALE AND BEYOND THE PALE

The Pale, the boundary that so fascinated young Con, was indeed a wall in places, just as Con imagined. More often, however, it was little more than a bank with a hedge on top. It stretched from Dublin right up to Roches Castle, (which you should visit) where the children were so nearly captured. Nevertheless it was an important boundary. Inside the Pale lived the English, and people who were prepared to live under English rule. Here, for example, you would have to attend a Protestant church every Sunday, so Catholics were excluded. Outside the Pale, however, the native Irish and the old Norman families could attend Mass on Sundays, and live under a mixture of English and Irish (Brehon) laws. The Norman families kept closer links to English ways than would the native Irish. Sinéad was christened Jane until Uncle Hugh gave her the Irish version of her name. Likewise, when James changed his name to the Irish, Séamus, this was symbolic for him.

TIME AND WEATHER

Our story takes place between the actual dates of the Flight of the Earls, starting on Saturday, 8 September 1607 when Hugh O'Neill bade a tearful farewell to his old friend Garret Moore at Mellifont, through to Friday, 14 September when the boat sailed. I had to fit the children's search for Con to this timetable. I tried to do the same with the weather. We know that Hugh and Catherine struggled through heavy rain while crossing the Sperrin mountains. So this is the rain that Sinéad hears beating on the O'Brolchain tent that same night. Likewise, the storm that I have driving the French ship, *St Lucia*, into Portsalon, was at that time driving O'Neill's ship past Arranmore island, in Donegal, where we know he had hoped to stop for supplies.

A LITTLE HISTORY

THE IRISH, THE NORMANS, AND THE ENGLISH

At this time there were three main groups of people all fighting for Irish soil. First the ancient Irish, like Hugh O'Neill. Secondly the Normans, like our de Cashel family, who had come to Ireland four hundred years earlier and were now as Irish as the Irish. And third the English, who were pushing out from the Pale, taking Irish and Norman land and forcing Catholics to become Protestants. (Note: the Normans are sometimes referred to as the 'Old English', but I use 'Norman' in this book.)

ENGLISH INVASION & NORMAN REBELLION

Since the time of the Norman invasion of 1169, English kings had been trying to conquer Ireland. But the Irish clans were strong and warlike, and the invaders made little progress. Then King Henry VIII made a clever offer, namely, that if the Irish chiefs surrendered, he would grant or 'lend' them back their land, give them English titles, and protect them from their enemies. Many of the Irish chiefs fell for this offer. Henry called this *Surrender and Re-grant*. However, under Irish law the land belongs to the clan, not to the chief! As the English anticipated, the clans now turned on their own chiefs. This was an early example of *Divide and Rule* (making your enemies fight among themselves, so that they don't fight you). Some of the great Norman/Irish families, however, rebelled against the English. In the Desmond Rebellion that followed, huge tracts of Munster were made uninhabitable and thousands of Irish and Norman lives were lost. Land that was not grabbed was 'planted,' that is, given to English settlers to farm.

YOUNG HUGH O'NEILL

When Hugh O'Neill was a young boy of nine, an English lord offered to foster him to his family in England. In this way Hugh got a good education and learned English customs and manners. Not surprisingly, when he was twenty-one years old, he found himself fighting on the side of the English, helping to put down the Desmond rebellion.

HUGH O'NEILL'S EIGHT-YEAR WAR

Nobody knows when Hugh realised that the English were not just destroying his country, but were threatening his own lands in Ulster. Gradually Hugh gathered the Ulster clans. Then, in 1595, he joined forces with his great friend Red Hugh O'Donnell and started a war against the English that was to last for eight years. Not since the time of Brian Boru had Ireland been so united. O'Neill's greatest victory was at the Battle of the Yellow Ford (near where the children crossed the

Blackwater river); his greatest defeat was at the Battle of Kinsale, where a small Spanish army had landed to help him. (It was here that I have Sinéad's father getting his wounded knee.) After this defeat, the clans began to break up and many, like the O'Cahans and MacSweeneys, sided with the English. Though O'Neill was pardoned, Chichester continued to hound him, and hunt down his people in Ulster. Eventually, the only thing O'Neill could do was to leave Ireland to get help from abroad. When he heard that a ship had arrived for him, and was waiting for him at Rathmullan, he sent out word to find his son Con and bring him to the ship. Con never did arrive.

CONQUEST ACHIEVED

These were ferocious times; the Irish as well as the English were capable of inhuman acts. However, the English invasion and conquest of Ireland was not simply a matter of England imposing new overlords on the native Irish, as the Normans had done, or changing the rule of law, but was achieved by extermination. Vast numbers of men, women and children were killed either by the sword or by hunger. The modern word, genocide, should not be used lightly, but the English wholesale slaughter of people whom they claimed as their own subjects was inexcusable. There were, however, many English officials and people who were opposed to these methods, and who tried to make peace and to mediate, but their voices were not heard.

The conquest of Ireland is of world significance. This was the birth of the colonial era, and for the next four hundred years the methods of colonisation developed in Ireland would be used by the colonial powers in their colonies throughout the world.

PLANTATIONS

Within ten years of the Flight of the Earls, Ulster would be divided up and given to largely decent, hard-working Scottish farmers who had no part in the dreadful deeds that had gone before them, and indeed knew little about them. The Plantation of Ulster was then complete.

SOME EXAMPLES FROM *FUGITIVES!*

When Sinéad is in despair at having to marry Bonmann, Father reminds her that her grandfather had signed away his lands to King Henry VIII (*Surrender and Re-grant*) so the castle didn't really belong to them. We have several examples of *Divide and Rule*, one of the most successful was Fenton's success in turning James against Fion, which of course resulted in their duel. On a larger scale, we have Chichester fomenting trouble between Sir Malachy and Hugh O'Neill by suggesting that Sir Malachy go out to steal his friend O'Neill's cattle. If Chichester had taken James as a hostage, he might have fostered him, like young Hugh, in order to indoctrinate him. Or, he might have thrown him into Dublin Castle and demanded a ransom that could have ruined Sir Malachy. It would have been a great temptation for Sir Malachy to marry off Sinéad to the wealthy and powerful Bonmann.

FAMILIES AND FRIENDS

GROWING UP

In the fifteenth century, childhood was over at the age of fourteen; life for the Castle children would soon change. In James's case, his future would be centred on the castle which he would soon inherit. Fion's future, in contrast, would have centred on shifting herds of cattle which he could spend his life defending from his neighbours. In Sinéad's case, she would be preparing a trousseau of clothes and linen for a marriage that her parents would arrange for her (hopefully with her consent).

FOSTER BROTHERS, CATTLE & THE VICTOR'S TOUCH

Fostering a son to another chief or family helped the young person's education but also helped bind families and allies together. I like to think that O'Neill's fostering of Con to the O'Brolchains was to give him the freedom he clearly needed. The bonds between fosterlings ran deep, so quarrels between foster brothers were serious. When James tried to steal O'Neill's cattle he was betraying not just O'Neill, but his own foster brother, Fion.

Duels were used to decide quarrels, most of which would end with surrender, not death. Therefore some ritual was necessary. The English would have shaken hands, but here something less English and more symbolic is needed. The 'victor's touch' is my invention.

POETS

Haystacks belongs to the Gaelic order of poets and lawyers. They came from privileged families and were made welcome wherever they went. No one wants a mocking song made about them. In this book Haystacks has attached himself to Hugh O'Neill and his family. He doesn't tell the children what to do, but encourages them to make their own decisions. He knows that the MacSweeneys trace their family back to Niall of the Nine Hostages, so he uses the story of Niall to shame The MacSweeney, the clan leader, into releasing the children.

The *Song of Amergin*, the poem that Haystacks recites for Sinead, is thought to be the oldest poem to have been written down in Irish. Amergin is said to have been a Milesian prince who came to Ireland before the time of Christ.

CHARACTERS FROM HISTORY

HUGH O'NEILL

Everyone agrees that Hugh O'Neill was a man of great charm. Hardened British soldiers like Mountjoy, who granted him his pardon after the Battle of Kinsale, fell under his spell. He was very emotional and would burst into tears when he felt strongly about something. He was also a brilliant soldier. He was married four times. When his second wife Siobhán died, he promptly eloped with Mabel Bagenal, the twenty-year-old sister of his arch enemy Sir Henry Bagenal. Sinéad would have remembered this story when Uncle Hugh pretended to elope with her. Hugh had grown-up children from previous marriages. Two of his younger children, John and Brian, were already on the ship at Rathmullan, and Catherine, his fourth wife, was pregnant. Nevertheless he took the risk of waiting for Con.

SIR ARTHUR CHICHESTER

Chichester could act as the perfect gentleman, at the same time as a ruthless soldier. A portrait of Sir Arthur shows him with a small, pointed beard, a downward-sweeping moustache and penetrating eyes. His deep hatred of O'Neill stemmed from when his brother was killed in a skirmish with one of O'Neill's allies. First under Lord Deputy Mountjoy, and later as Lord Deputy himself, Chichester developed a strategy of death and starvation in O'Neill's territory. He built a network of forts there and used these to spread death and destruction – anybody found alive, man, woman or child, was put to the sword; houses were burned, crops destroyed, and cattle taken, so that there was neither food nor shelter. Fion tells this to Sinéad in his famine nightmare. Today Chichester would be tried for war crimes. He had an extensive network of spies, like Fenton. He also persuaded a number of Irish chiefs to come over to the English cause, but then abandoned them when their usefulness was over; O'Cahan, for example, ended his life in the Tower of London.

OTHER CHARACTERS FROM HISTORY

The MacSweeneys went over to the English side shortly after the Battle of Kinsale. They could easily have betrayed O'Neill and his ship to the English, but did not. They did, however, refuse to provide provisions for the ship, which when it sailed, it had a hundred people on board. MacSweeney's son really did lead an attack on a party from the ship as they tried to fill their water barrels at a stream. There are also reports of O'Neill's followers doing some cattle stealing in order to get meat for the voyage.

Other historical characters are mere shadows. All we know of young Con's foster family is that they were semi-nomadic cattle herders, but when I found that the name O'Brolchain belonged to cattle herdsmen from County Tyrone, I felt I must use it.

Garret Moore, an English member of the Irish Privy Council, was also a personal friend of Hugh O'Neill. He lived at Mellifont, an abbey and castle which you can visit today. He is one of the nice men of Irish history. On several occasions he tried to act as peacemaker between O'Neill and the English. O'Neill was making a tearful farewell to his old friend when I have his son, John, arriving at the de Cashel castle to ask Sir Malachy for help in finding Con.

A CONFESSION

While making-up incidents for this book I have asked myself continually: 'Could this really have happened?' If the answer was 'no' then I had to leave it out. One exception is the gathering of the clans that Sinéad and Hugh remember when looking down from the battlements. There must, undoubtedly, have been such a gathering, before they set out for Kinsale, but it is unlikely to have happened so close to the Pale. Also, as the battle took place in December (1601), it would not have been such a splendid affair. However, I allowed it, as it was an opportunity to describe the soldiers of the time and also to allow Hugh to grieve over the huge number of men and friends who died in the battle.

Aubrey Flegg

For further information visit
The O'Brien Press website: www.obrien.ie